ART is Fun

Sally Henry

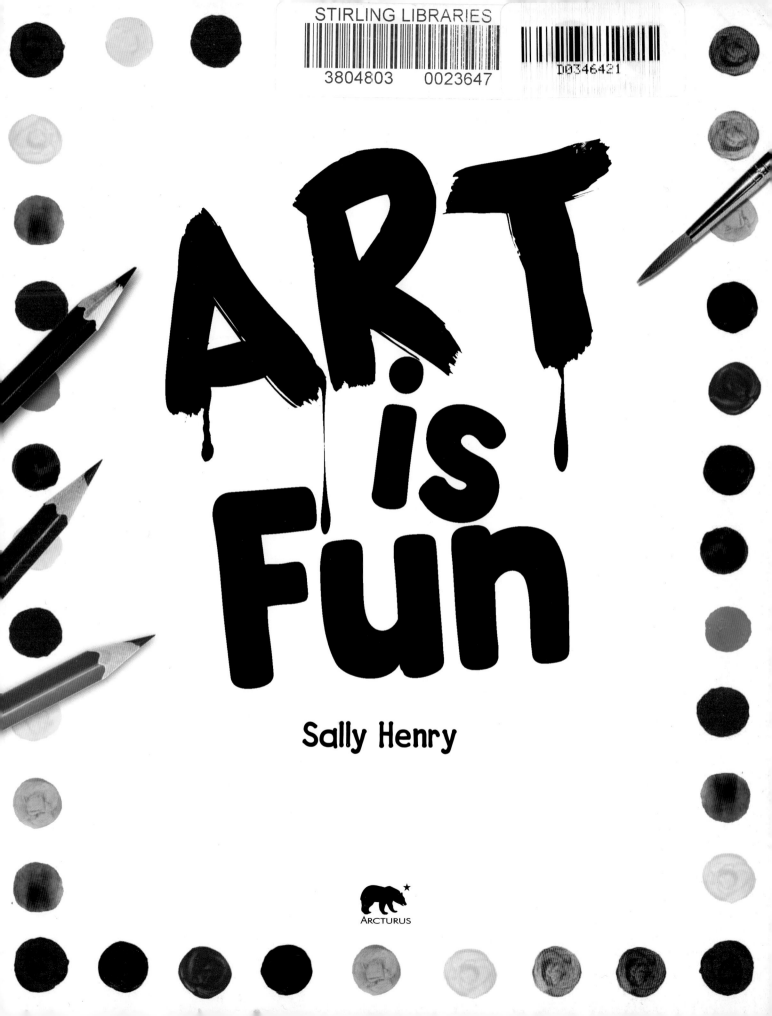

ARCTURUS

ARCTURUS

This edition published in 2011 by Arcturus Publishing Limited
26/27 Bickels Yard, 151–153 Bermondsey Street,
London SE1 3HA

Editor: Alex Woolf
Designers: Sally Henry and Trevor Cook
Consultant: Daisy Fearns
Original photography: Sally Henry and Trevor Cook

Every attempt has been made to clear copyright.
Should there be any inadvertent omission,
please apply to the publisher for rectification.

ISBN: 978-1-84837-375-4
CH001146EN

Printed in China

Contents

Introduction

Drawing

All artists need to be able to draw. Drawing is the best way to work out your ideas, whether you are using paint, fabric, paper, card or modelling clay. A drawing can be a first step, or even a finished piece.

Pencils for drawing are made of graphite – a kind of compressed carbon. They're marked with H for hard, or B for soft (black). An H is just a little harder than average; a 6H is very hard indeed. Soft pencils are great for drawing and give a greater range of tones than hard ones. Keep a clean **eraser** and a good-quality **sharpener** handy.

Charcoal gives great tonal range, but it can be messy, so handle with care. Use with a **soft** or **putty eraser**. Soft pencil and charcoal should be 'fixed' with **fixative** – a kind of aerosol varnish.

Marker pens come with waterproof or water-soluble inks that can each give quite different results.

Coloured pencils work best on paper with a slightly textured surface. But they're not as good for drawing as plain graphite pencils.

Wax crayons are great to use with water-colour paint. You can draw with ordinary **wax candles**, too.

Papers come in lots of different colours and textures. Keep your best papers for drawings you are going to spend some time on. Drawings with clean lines in pencil or ink need a smooth surface. Soft pencils, coloured crayons and charcoal work well with a slightly textured surface.

Making marks

See how many different kinds of **marks** you can make using a soft pencil.

When you draw shapes, try to make your lines describe what you are drawing. **Shading** makes the round shape below more like a ball. It can cast a shadow, too.

Use **texture** to show what something is made of.

Frame your view

Cut a hole about 180mm x 130mm (7in x 5in) in a piece of stout card. Hold it up to frame your view. You can mark a piece of transparent plastic with grid lines to make it easy to position things in your **viewfinder**.

Perspective

vanishing point

We can use **perspective** to draw space, inside and outside. A road or rail track running directly away from us shows the **vanishing point** on the horizon.

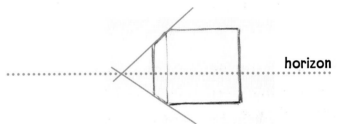

horizon

The cube above is an example of **one-point perspective**. The lines in the picture converge at the vanishing point.

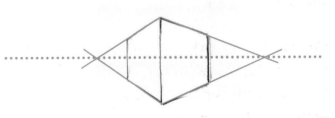

This **two-point perspective** shows the cube at an angle to the viewer. There are two vanishing points.

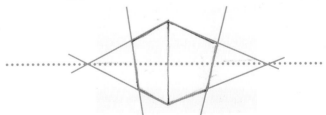

A **three-point perspective** is the most realistic of all but more difficult to set up. Here, the horizon and construction lines converge outside the frame.

Painting

We've used **poster paints** and **ready-mixed paints** for the projects in this book. You can apply them thick, straight from the pot, or add water to thin them.

Brushes can be expensive, so it's important to try as many as you can before you buy your own.

You'll need a large brush for painting areas of colour, and a smaller one for detailed work. Soft brushes work best with the kind of paint we are going to use.

You can buy various **pots** and **palettes** for holding your water and mixing colour. We like mixing our paint on old white plates, and we put our water in old mugs or yogurt pots!

Colour

You can get good results with just a few basic colours. On the right is a selection of colours mixed from just six different pots – **magenta, yellow, cyan, red, green and blue**. Keep your paints clean when you mix colours. Always wash your brush when you change colours.

6

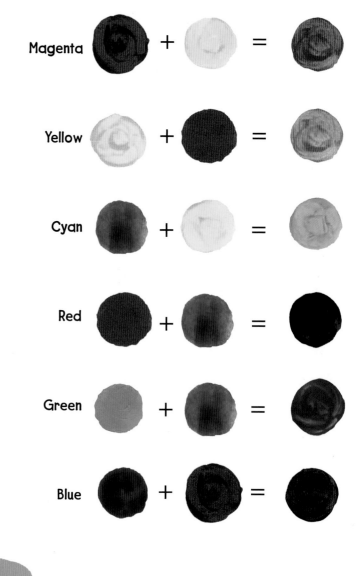

Magenta + =

Yellow + =

Cyan + =

Red + =

Green + =

Blue + =

Light and dark

Adding white to your colour makes a **tint**.

Adding black makes a **shade**.

Use light and shade with colour to make things more solid.

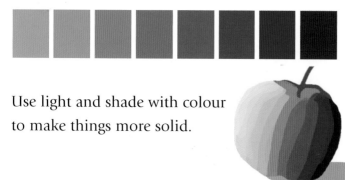

Collage

'Collage' comes from the French word for glue. It's all about sticking different things together to make pictures. You can use glue stick, craft glue, or universal glue, depending on the materials you are using.

When you discover some interesting things together in one place, you may also find that they work well together in a collage.

Collecting materials

You can make your collage out of almost anything. Start off with different materials you can find in and around your home. Look out for colour, texture and pattern. Always make sure you ask if you can use whatever it is you find! Here's a short list of things to collect.

- **coloured and printed paper** – newspapers, magazines, wrapping paper, junk mail, postcards, old tickets
- **fabric** – dressmaking material scraps, knitting wool
- **plastics** – plastic bags, drinking straws, containers and lids, packaging
- **natural things** – dried leaves, twigs, seeds, flowers, tree bark, grasses, feathers
- **dried foods** – peas and beans, grains, pasta shapes
- **things from the seashore** – driftwood, shells, small pebbles.

Shaping your work

You can create exciting effects when you tear, rather than cut paper or card. Make the softer torn edge part of the picture. Make straight tears by folding first, then pulling apart along the crease. The main thing with all these materials is to experiment!

Paper folding

Paper was invented a long time ago in the East, and there are many ancient paper-folding designs. Old and new designs all share the same basic requirements for success.

Paper for folding can be ordinary-quality, coloured office-copier type A4-size, unless the instructions say otherwise. It's fun to use all sorts of paper, though. Try patterned paper, such as wrapping paper. It's usually printed on one side and plain white on the other side. Coloured art paper comes in sizes much bigger than office paper, so it's good for a special project.

To make our paper flowers, you can use either tissue paper or crêpe paper.

Tissue paper comes in bright colours. It is thin enough to let light shine through it, making the colours bright but natural looking.

Crêpe paper is thicker than tissue paper and has lots of tiny creases. This means that by gently pulling at it, you can stretch the paper so that it's no longer flat, but bent into a curve. We have used crêpe paper to make the petals of the flower, above.

Fold

The dotted line shows where the fold should be made. The arrow shows the direction in which to make the fold. There is usually an edge or a point that the folded part has to meet.

Crease

Fold a sheet of paper and then open it out again. The mark left behind is a crease. Depending on the design, you can use this as a fold later in the construction, or you might just use it as a guide to get other folds in the right place.

Burnished fold

When you want a fold to be really crisp and flat, or a crease to be very clear, use a tool to burnish it. Make the fold very carefully, and check it is accurate. Then gently press down along the fold using a tool such as a ruler or the back of a spoon.

Stick paper to paper with a **glue stick**. Put the paper to be glued face down on clean scrap paper and apply the glue evenly, working towards the edge.

Universal glue that comes in a tube is best for sticking odd-shaped bits together, and for sticking paper to other materials.

Card making

A **greetings card** is always more welcome when it has been made by the person sending it. In this book you'll find lots of ways to make your cards even more special.

You need a supply of coloured **paper** and **card**. All sizes are useful, but you may need larger pieces of paper to make the special, oversized envelopes.

Make larger cards from thicker material so they stand up properly.

Envelopes

For most projects, an ordinary envelope will do for your card. You can get coloured and unusually shaped envelopes in some craft shops. If you want a particular size and you can't find it, try making your own using this simple guide. In the picture we've shown the shape of the paper (orange) you will need to make the envelope (red). You can adapt this design to make different shapes of envelope.

Finish the envelope as follows:
- Fold the bottom flap up.
- Fold the side flaps, glue their lower edges and stick down to the bottom flap.
- Fold the top flap down.

Don't stick the top flap down until you have put your card inside!

Presentation

It's great to be able to give your friends a beautiful, unusual or funny greetings card that you've made yourself. There are lots of designs to choose from in this book, including shaped and three-dimensional as well as conventional ones. You can use paint, pens or collage to make your cards.

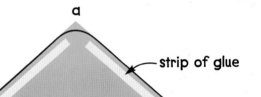

Design

It's important that your finished card fit its envelope, so it's a good idea to have the envelope ready before you start work on the card.

a

— strip of glue

c

The red shape is the size of the inside of your envelope. Put it in the middle of the diamond.

d

b

Distance a to b is twice the height of the red shape plus 25mm (1in). Distance c to d is twice the width of the red shape plus 25mm (1in).

Clay modelling

Some clay, a few simple tools and your imagination are all you need to have fun with modelling. We use a special coloured clay called polymer clay. It comes in lots of great colours and hardens well when baked in an oven.

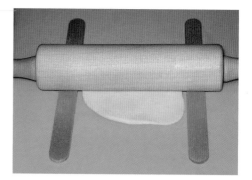

Preparation

Polymer clay sticks to itself very well. It's also quite easy to stick things to it. Unfortunately, it can also stick in the wrong places – so keep it clear of expensive carpets! If there's no cooking going on, the kitchen might be the best place to work. Cover your worktop with a plastic sheet (a plastic carrier bag is ideal). Hold the sheet in place with sticky tape.

Start by kneading the clay in your hands. This way you make sure it's the same consistency right through. Kneading also warms and softens the clay, making it easier to mould or roll out.

Tools like the ones below are from a craft shop. We found our rolling pin in a junior cooking set. Flat lolly sticks come free with ice lollies!

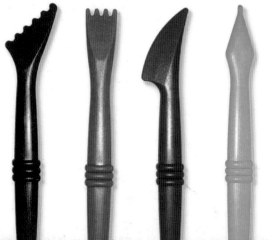

To make a **flat sheet**, take some clay and roll it out with the rolling pin. Lolly sticks placed either side of the clay help to keep an even thickness.

We often need **coils**, (long, even cylinders of clay) to make objects such as pots. Take a ball of clay and make it into a sausage shape in your hands. Roll it out into a long, thin shape on your work surface, using just your fingers.

Hardening

Polymer clay is hardened by baking in an ordinary oven. You must ask an adult to help you with this.

DO NOT USE A MICROWAVE OVEN!

The oven temperature should be around 130°C (275°F) but be sure to read the manufacturer's instructions that come with the clay for the correct baking time and temperature. Bake your clay models in an ovenproof dish. Allow plenty of time for cooling before you take the clay out of the dish. Be patient, it's worth the wait!

Drawing

Portraits

Drawing faces is an excellent way to start having fun with art. Ask a friend to sit for you, and tell him or her how long you will take to do your drawing. Try short poses as well as long ones. Adapt your style to the time you have. The drawing on the left took half-an-hour. The one on the right took one minute.

You will need:

- *Tinted or white drawing paper*
- *Soft pencils, 2B, 6B*
- *Coloured pencils or pastels*
- *Marker pens, white chalk*
- *Soft eraser*

30 MINUTES

What to do...

Drawing 1 is done using a soft brown pencil with white chalk on tinted paper with a textured surface. Drawing 2 is done with a marker pen on smooth white paper. If you can't get anyone to model for you, use a mirror to draw a picture of yourself.

2 MINUTES

12

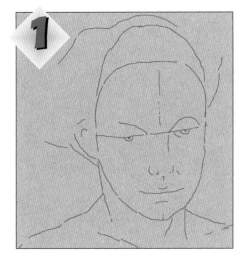

Fix your paper to a board. Build up the head, hair, neck and shoulders in soft brown pencil.

Use a brown pencil to draw in the hair, eyes, eyebrows and nose. Add some shading for the cheeks, mouth and chin.

Use white chalk for the highlights and to lighten the background.

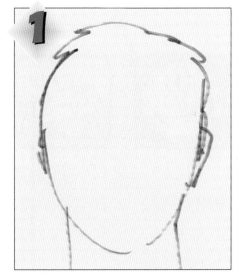

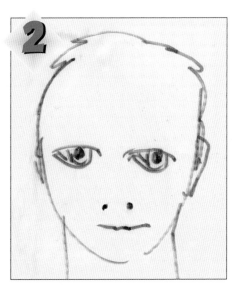

Look very carefully and judge the shape of the head. Try to draw the shape in one go.

Mark in the pupils of the eyes, then draw the eyes and eyelids. Put dots for the nostrils and just a single line for the mouth.

Sketch in the hairline and the eyebrows. Draw in the shape of the nose, then add lines to complete the mouth.

My friend

As your drawing skills develop, more friends might agree to be models for you. Ask one of them to sit for ten minutes. It will seem a long time to them, so you will have to work fast!

10
MINUTES

2
MINUTES

You will need:

- *Drawing paper*
- *Soft pencil, fine marker pen*
- *Coloured pencils or wax crayons*
- *Eraser*

What to do...

Organize your paper, drawing board and pencils before your friend arrives. Provide a comfortable chair in a position with good light. When the model is seated, explain that he or she must keep as still as possible for ten minutes. It is useful to have a clock in the room, so you can both see the time. We got our model to relax by listening to music.

Study the model carefully. Check the proportions of the body. Use a soft pencil to sketch in some simple outline shapes.

Work quickly and lightly to draw in the features and the hairstyle. Rub out any lines you don't need. Keep looking at the model to make sure your drawing is accurate.

Use a fine marker pen to develop your drawing. Here we've added more details to the hair, the headphones and the jewellery.

With a coloured pencil or wax crayon, add shading for the skin colour.

We used a dark crayon to add texture to the chair so that it contrasts with the clothes.

Hints and tips

- Sign and date your drawing and record the name of your model.
- Experiment with different pencils, markers pens and crayons to get textures.
- Store your work flat in a folder or large drawer.
- Keep a sketch book.

Young animal

Horses are many people's favourite animal. The horse pictured is a Shire foal and is not too difficult to draw.

You will need:

- *Drawing paper*
- *Pencils, marker pens*
- *Eraser*
- *Colouring materials*

20 MINUTES

What to do...

Set up your drawing board and study step 1. Copy the shapes on to your paper in soft pencil.

5 MINUTES

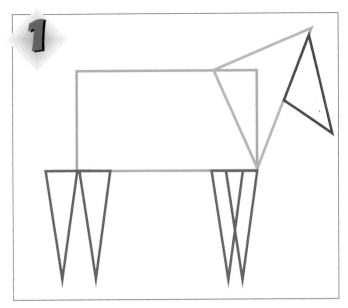

1

Start with the blue rectangle, then draw four triangles for legs. A green triangle shows the neck and a red triangle shows the head.

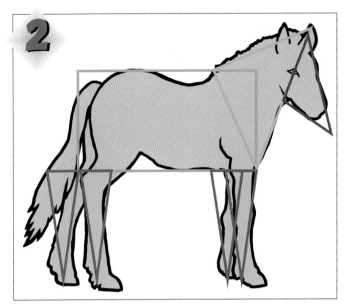

2

Now draw the outline of the foal in pencil over your collection of shapes. When you have got it right, go over the outline with a big marker pen. Rub out the pencil shapes.

3

Add fine marker pen lines to show the mane, ears, nose, nostrils and mouth. Draw in the hooves and fetlocks. Colour in all areas.

4

This close-up shows how to colour in the eye and add the highlight. Use colouring pens, pencils or crayons to complete your picture.

Still-life study

25 MINUTES

5 MINUTES

Drawing a fashionable item of clothing can often produce interesting results. Here is a picture of a much-loved trainer. We've used blue-coloured pencil with some coloured crayons and a marker pen.

You will need:

- *An item to draw*
- *Drawing paper*
- *Pencils*
- *Eraser*
- *Coloured pencils or crayons*
- *Thick marker pen*

What to do...

Take your time to get the proportions right at the beginning. If your object has natural divisions or surface patterns, like our trainer, include these in your initial drawing. They help to establish its form.

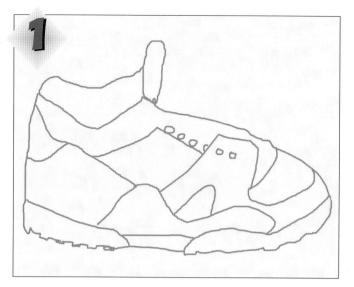

Make your drawing large. There's plenty of detail to fill a bigger piece of paper.

We decided to work with several different shades of blue. The shading picks up the uneven surface of the paper and adds interest.

Try out some of the different effects you can get with your colours.

Vary the angle of your shading to give texture. To complete the drawing, use your darkest blue on the sole and the seams. Observational studies like this will help to train your eye.

Try using rough - textured or tinted paper for your drawings.

Cartoons

Cartoons are fun to draw because they have simple lines and you can use any colours you like. Our cartoon shows a hippo visiting a waterhole with her calf. Baby hippos are just a smaller version of the adults, but without the huge teeth!

You will need:

- Paper
- Soft pencil
- Thick, black marker pen
- Coloured marker pens or paints and a brush

20
MINUTES

What to do...

Cartoon characters need some basic features to give them personality. Our hippo has a round shape, stumpy teeth and a cheeky eye!

5
MINUTES

1

Draw generous rounded shapes in soft pencil.

2

Use the rounded shapes to create the body outline.

3

Use a thick marker pen to draw a strong image.

4

Add some colour with paint or marker pens.
Draw a waterhole background
(see opposite page).

Jointed
wooden
animal figure

We've used the
model to practice
drawing an animal
in motion

Try drawing the
animal in different
positions

Jungle wildlife

You may not have seen a real jungle, but that doesn't matter. You can let your imagination take flight with this colourful drawing!

You will need:

- *Card or paper*
- *Coloured markers, soft pencil*
- *Coloured pencils or crayons*
- *Nature books, magazines*

40
MINUTES

What to do...

To fnd out what the animals you want to draw look like, search for their pictures in nature books and magazines. Or you can use your imagination to create a jungle for your animals!

10
MINUTES

1 We have created a jungle background and drawn a few unusual animals to live there. You can make your own jungle and choose the animals you want to paint.

Start by drawing in some outlines of bushes and other plants in soft pencil. Add grass areas, jungle paths, a stream and a pool.

 2 We found it was useful to draw and colour in our animals first. Then we drew over our pencil jungle outlines with coloured markers. This helped show the areas where we wanted to put certain colours.

We filled in the lighter colours first, adding the dark areas of background last.

Here are some more animals you might find in the jungle, though perhaps not the crazy-coloured rhino!

Fantasy figure

15 MINUTES

5 MINUTES

Here's another challenge for your imagination – think of a fantasy figure to draw.

You will need:

- *Drawing paper*
- *Soft pencil, eraser*
- *Marker pens, coloured pencils*
- *Paint brushes, paints or coloured inks*

What to do...

Follow steps 1–6 to draw our fantasy wizard and his cat. He would look wonderful as a big poster image. Try to find a really large sheet of paper for this drawing.

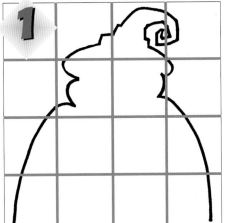

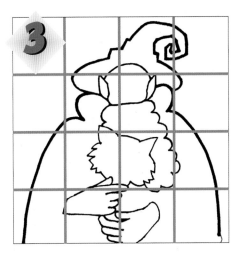

Draw a grid of sixteen squares on a photocopy of the picture opposite. Make a similar grid on your paper. Start your drawing using a pencil. When you reach step 5, use a black marker pen to draw bold lines on top of your pencil.

Add the face shape and ears. See how his collar becomes visible now that his head is outlined. Look carefully at the big picture opposite to help with the details.

Join his beard to his face. Copy the position of his hands, using the grid to guide you. Draw the outline of the cat between his beard and his hands.

Draw in the wizard's eyes and nose. Notice how they are joined together! Put in lines for the sides of the cat's body.

Look again at the large drawing. Add the eyebrows, curls on the beard, the cat's face and whiskers, the bangles, rings and details on the wizard's hat.

Add the stars and moons, then use flat colour to fill in the line drawing. Use marker pens, coloured pencils, paints or inks. Make the wizard really colourful and fantastical!

Racing cars

Most people like the look of stylish, fast cars. They may seem quite hard to draw, but if you make a grid on a photograph or do a careful tracing, you can achieve impressive results.

You will need:

- *Photograph of your car*
- *Soft pencil (B–2B), eraser*
- *Smooth paper*
- *Large-tip black marker pen*
- *Fine-point black marker pen*
- *White chalk*

15
MINUTES

What to do...

Look through some car magazines. You need a picture that shows the whole car. We've cut ours out from its background to make it clearer.

5
MINUTES

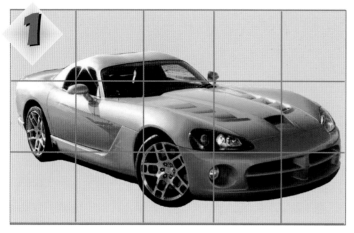

Draw a grid of squares on your photo. Draw a matching grid of faint pencil lines on your paper.

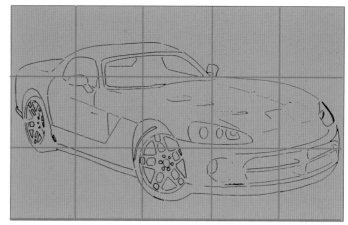

Alternatively, you can trace the outline. Using a light touch with your pencil, draw the basic shape.

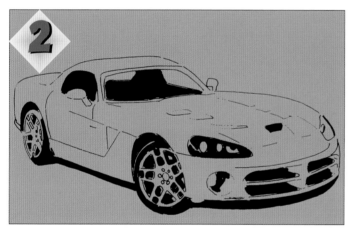

Use a marker pen to add in the dark areas in black. Use a fine black marker to add the details.

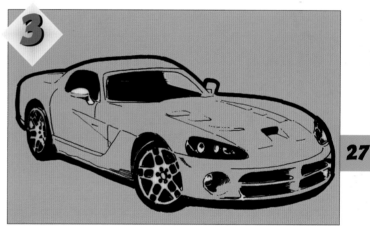

Use white chalk to show the shiny parts. Put a thick outline round the outside of the car.

Try working the other way round, with another car. Use coloured paper. Draw a thick outline round the car first. Use a grid to help you.

Use your fine black marker for the details. Add some reflection lines on the windscreen in white chalk. Shade in the tyres.

Manga faces

Drawing in the manga style takes years of practice, but here are a few helpful ideas to get you started. We've chosen a boy and a girl to draw. We've also shown five steps for drawing a manga eye. Follow this method when you ink in your work with marker pens.

You will need:

- *Your favourite manga stories*
- *Paper, soft pencil, eraser*
- *Marker pens, coloured pencils*
- *Paints and paintbrushes*

25 MINUTES

What to do...

Look through your manga books. Study the difference between various artists' styles. They all have their own way of showing their subjects' characters.

5 MINUTES

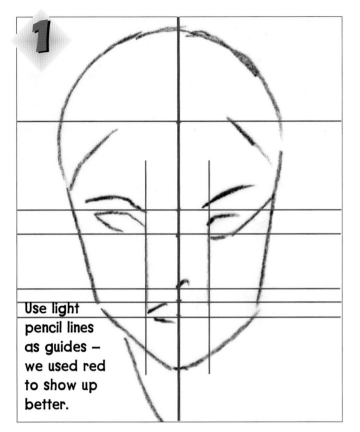

1

Use light pencil lines as guides – we used red to show up better.

Use a pencil to draw an oval for the girl's head. Put lines to show where the eyes and mouth go.

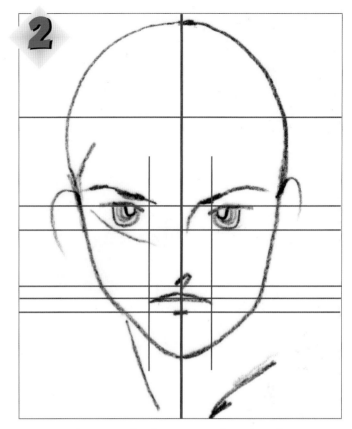

2

Start to draw in the basic eye shapes. The eyes are the most important feature of a manga face.

3

This girl has very short hair. Work out the style.

4

Add more pencil detail; finish with markers.

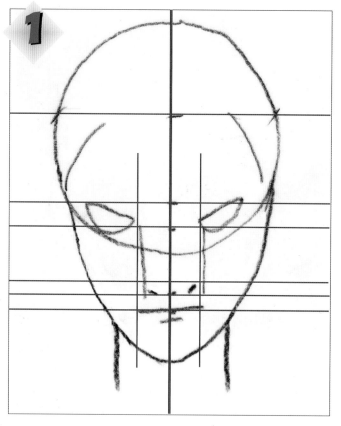

Use a pencil to draw an oval for the boy's head. Add lines for where the eyes and mouth go.

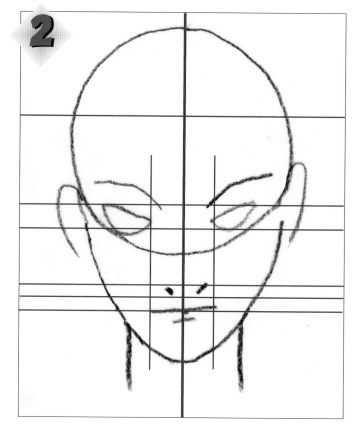

Draw in the basic features. The eyes are an important feature. His eyes are on a slant.

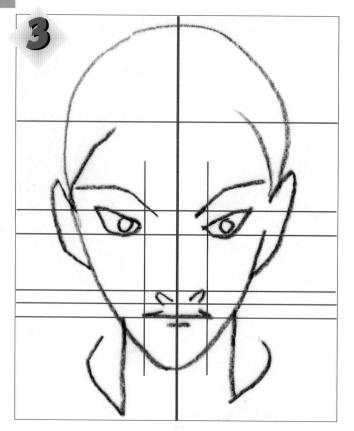

The boy has spiky, long hair and looks elfin.

Add more details in pencil. Finish with markers.

Painting

Self-portrait

Painting a good self-portrait is a skill that takes lots of practice. Learn how to be your own model!

45 MINUTES

10 MINUTES

You will need:

- *Cartridge paper, drawing board, tape, pins*
- *Paints and mixing palette*
- *Brushes, round 3mm, 6mm and flat 12mm (0.125in, 0.25in and 0.5in)*
- *Wall or table mirror*

What to do...

Make sure your mirror is firmly fixed and at the right height. Attach the paper to the board with tape or pins. Sit in front of the mirror with your board so you can comfortably see both your reflection and your drawing without moving your head. Is there enough light for you to see properly?

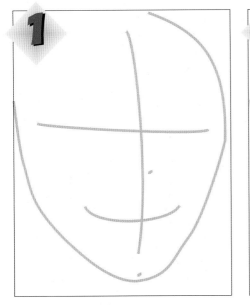

Lightly draw the shape of your head. Halfway down, draw a guideline for your eyes, then one for your mouth. Put in a centre line. Put dots for the tip of your nose and your chin.

Mix some thick paint to make a skin colour. Using a 6mm (0.25in) brush, paint in the shape of your eyes, mouth, nose, face and neck. Look very carefully at your eyes in the mirror.

Using a small brush, paint in your eye colour. Put black dots in the centre for the pupils. A tiny white highlight dot will make your eyes look more lifelike.

33

Model your skin colour in three shades. Touch in your lips, then use a bigger brush to paint your hair. Add hair colours: dark first, then texture with lighter colours.

Add detail to your mouth and teeth. Use dark hair colour for eyebrows and eyelashes. Be careful – you can change your expression with these!

Check details . . . tidy up. Well done – it's finished!

Simple still life

Artists through the ages have used still life to experiment with different ways of painting. Here we are using still life to explore colour.

35 MINUTES

10 MINUTES

You will need:

- Cartridge paper
- Soft pencil, ruler
- Paints, mixing palette and water
- Brushes, 6mm, 12mm and 25mm (0.125in, 0.25in and 0.5in)
- Objects to make an arrangement

What to do...

Set up your group of objects in a good light. We've chosen plain backgrounds and strong colours for our first still life. Use your viewfinder frame to check your composition. Place your paper so that you can work and look directly at your group of objects. Draw a large square on your paper in pencil to mark out the shape of your painting.

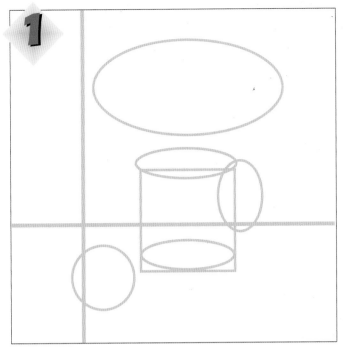

Our composition seems to fit well in the square shape. Sketch the objects in the painting using simple outlines only.

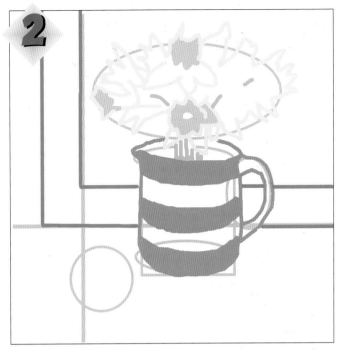

We are using the edge of a window to make a big L-shape in the background. It helps to frame the arrangement. Next, we sketch in the flowers and the jug.

This picture is all flat shapes, but we can use the outline to describe the different things in it. Paint the table, wall and window with flat colours.

Keep your edges crisp and colours clear. Give the picture interest by adding extra detail to the flowers to make them stand out among all the flat shapes.

Landscape

40 MINUTES

10 MINUTES

36

Landscape is what you can see outdoors, but it doesn't have to be the countryside. A town or city view is a landscape too, and it can be just as interesting to paint. There are also natural scenes to paint in parks and gardens.

You will need:

- *Card or paper, tissues*
- *Paint, mixing palette and water*
- *Brushes, round 3mm, 6mm and flat 12mm (0.125in, 0.25in and 0.5in)*
- *Card to make a framing window*

What to do...

Find a view that interests you. You may start from a photograph, but it's often more interesting to start with the real thing. Use the framing window to find a good composition in the landscape. We chose our view for its bright colours and unusual patterns.

Look carefully at your composition. Try to see the pattern in the landscape. Sometimes it helps to screw up your eyes to blur the view so that you can't see detail. Outline the patches of colour with light grey paint and a fine brush. Put in key details such as trees.

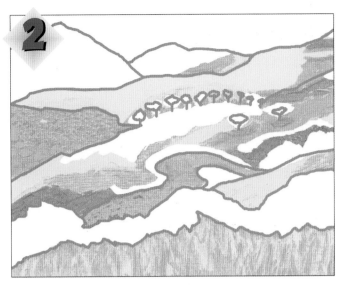

Start filling in the shapes. Paint the light colours first. Don't worry about painting over your drawing lines. You can give a feeling of depth by making colours more washed out towards the horizon. Build up the trees and bushes with light and dark greens.

Use light blue to create the sky. Add darker blue as required. If your sky has clouds, you can leave the paper unpainted to show up as white shapes. Paint landscapes in settled weather conditions to avoid the light changing.

Our picture was painted in the early evening when the hills looked very pink. Add darker colours last, to show shadows under trees, for example. Make a note of where and when you made the painting.

Dinosaur

Get up close to one of history's most terrifying beasts! Use a toy dinosaur as a model.

You will need:

- *Model dinosaur*
- *Pencil, coloured markers*
- *Drawing paper*
- *Paints, brushes and water*

20 MINUTES

What to do...

Position your model dinosaur against a plain background. We used a T-Rex, but you can use any models you have at home.

5 MINUTES

Here is a photo of our model. There's lots of detail. We can choose which bits to paint.

Make a pencil drawing of the head. Check the angle by looking at your model. Draw in his teeth, then carefully position his eye.

Use a black marker to draw over your pencil lines and make textures.

Paint in the background areas. We used blues and greens for the land, but try out any colours you like – it's great fun!

Creatures

All sorts of creatures bring colour into the world. Let's celebrate our favourite animal by making a painting of it.

35 MINUTES

10 MINUTES

You will need:

- Cartridge paper or thin card
- Paper varnish
- Black marker pens, soft pencil
- Paint, mixing palette and water
- Brushes, round 3mm, 6mm and flat 12mm (0.125in, 0.25in and 0.5in)
- Magazines, scissors

What to do...

Find a photograph of an animal or bird that you can draw on. For our picture, we've chosen to paint just the macaw's head and body. We are using the top half of our photo. You can trim your photo to improve the design for your painting. Draw a grid of squares on it.

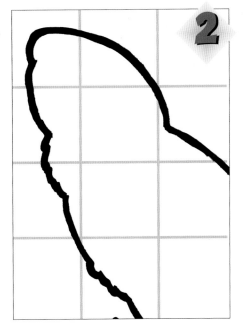

1

Our photo divides neatly into four squares vertically and three squares horizontally.

2

On the painting paper, draw similar squares – they can be bigger to fit the paper. Now draw the outline. The grid helps to place it accurately.

3

Next, use a fine pen to draw in all the smaller shapes. Be careful to get the eye in the right place.

4

Once you have drawn round all the different feathers, you can start colouring them.

5

If your model is brightly coloured like our parrot, you need to keep your colours clear and bright, too! Finish off with some clear paper varnish.

If you have a pet...

Make a big drawing in marker pen, then paint it!

Pop-art posters

55 MINUTES

5 MINUTES

Most portraits are painted in realistic tones, but with pop art you can go wild with colour!

You will need:

- *Card, paper, tracing paper, tissues*
- *Black marker pens, soft pencil, photocopier*
- *Magazine pictures or a photograph*
- *Black wax crayon, paints, brushes and water*

What to do...

You could work with a model for this project. Otherwise use a photo or magazine picture. Try to get A3-size photocopies to paint. The four pictures together will be very impressive.

Make a line drawing or tracing from a good photograph.

Outline the features, hair and some details of clothing.

Make four big photocopies and paint in the areas with colour.

Purple, orange and green are unlikely but interesting colours!

Blue, green and purple are cool colours.

Green, yellow and pink result in an unearthly complexion!

Make a line drawing from a photograph or model. Transfer your drawing to four separate sheets of paper by using tracing paper or a photocopier.

Use a black wax crayon to draw over the outlines on each copy. Try to follow your original lines, but don't worry if it's not that accurate.

Colour the four pictures differently, as on page 44. The wax crayon will resist the paint and make it easy to colour in the drawing. Differences in the finished paintings add interest.

These are some of the warm colours we used.

House of wax

Painting buildings is quite a challenge. We've chosen to paint one looking straight on, with plenty of detail but without very much depth. We have scaled-up the drawing from a small reference picture and used a wax resist effect on dark paper. Are you ready to have a go?

You will need:

40 MINUTES

- Dark-coloured paper
- Drawing pad or board
- Tape or drawing pins, tissues
- White pencil, ruler
- Paints and mixing palette
- Brushes, round 3mm, 6mm and 12mm (0.125in, 0.25in and 0.5in)
- Photocopy of reference picture
- Wax candle
- Washing-up liquid

What to do...

10 MINUTES

Use a photocopy of your picture. Fix your dark paper to your drawing board. Follow the steps to create the grids. Move from square to square, transferring the main structure lines from the reference to your work. Experiment with wax and paint mixed with washing-up liquid to get great texture effects.

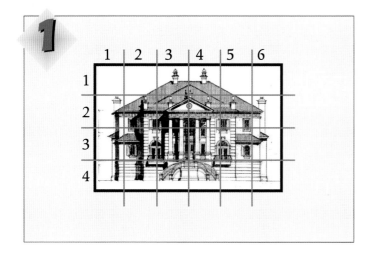

Use a photocopy reference smaller than your work. Draw a grid of squares on the reference.

Draw the same number of squares, but larger, on your paper. Draw lightly in white pencil.

47

In each square, copy the outlines in grey paint. When dry, go over the outlines with a candle.

Paint your house with thinned paint. The colour should run off the waxy lines.

Mixing washing-up liquid with your paint produces interesting effects.

We've filled in the sky with blue, but you can leave it as dark paper colour if you prefer.

Magic palace

We've painted an imaginary palace, full of colour, with an exotic garden. Follow our way of building up a painting, or create your own in a similar way.

The magic palace is a painting full of busy patterns. Look at the enlarged details in colour. We have made simple line drawings of the patterns.

Before you start your own magic palace, try drawing some patterns in line. Paint them in with colours you

like. This is the time to experiment. When you find a set of colours that look good together,

keep them for your next painting.

To add to the textures, we have painted over dry colour with more detail. You can do this too. We have also used a fine, metallic gold marker to outline some parts of the

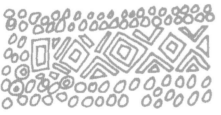

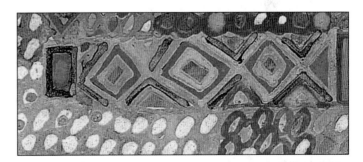

painting. It gives it a really rich result. Try experimenting to create your own effects.

49

Plan your painting by doing a line drawing of your palace.

Using another colour, draw in some plants in the garden and some people.

Paint in the background of the painting. Use flat colours to fill in the shapes you've drawn.

Add further interest to the picture by putting in more and more detail and texture.

Collage

The office car

This project is all about looking at things in a new way. Most homes have a collection of office bits and pieces somewhere. We've made ours into a car! See what you can find at home to make your own car.

You will need:

- *Coloured paper, scissors*
- *Cardboard, silver paper*
- *Paper clips, an old CD*
- *Universal glue*
- *Any small stationery items, such as: clips, lids, tags, paper fasteners, picture hooks, staples, split rings*

15 MINUTES

What to do...

2 MINUTES

Use coloured paper for the background. We've listed all the bits we started with, but yours may well be different. Decide from the things you collect which ones most look like part of a car. Remember to ask an adult before you take anything!

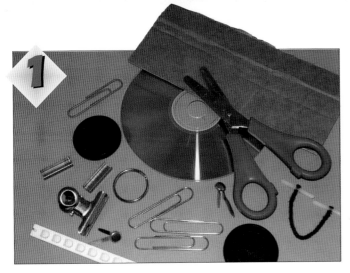

1 Check that you can have the old CD before you stick it down! We only need half of it to show, so cover the rest with the cardboard car shape.

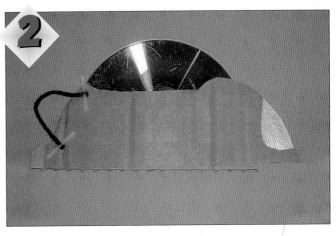

2 A patch of silver paper goes behind the headlight. The treasury tag makes a good luggage strap.

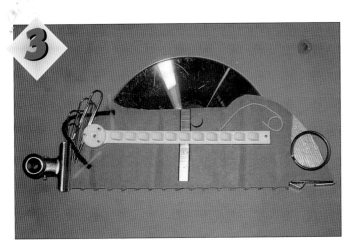

3 The paper clips are luggage. The bulldog clip becomes a tow-bar. Glue a tack on the door for a handle. Stick down the plastic picture hook bar to define the side panels and put the brass picture hook at the front for a bumper.

4 The split ring makes the headlamp. Wheels are made from plastic lids with paper fasteners opened and stuck down. We added a pink paper clip for an aerial. Your car is ready for the road!

Hints and tips

- Start with something striking. You don't have to do very much to these pieces of hardware to make a funny picture!

Textures

35 MINUTES

5 MINUTES

You will need:

- White paper, thin card, scissors, glue stick
- Pencil, marker pen, paints, brush, tissues
- Old magazines or felt

What to do...

To create a collage like this, you need to use
a range of painted or printed textures.
You could even use felt or other fabrics.

Either paint the pieces of felt different colours or cut out small pieces from magazines.

Do a simple line drawing on card as a guide.

Cut out shapes and stick them on the background.

Add figures or animals to complete your collage.

Fun gardening

Whatever the weather, you can make a lovely garden for yourself, indoors.

You will need:

- Coloured card
- Different kinds of leaves
- Seed heads or grasses
- Flower buds, twigs
- Scissors, universal glue
- Marker pen
- Wax crayons

40 MINUTES

What to do...

Collect basic materials from your garden or local park. You can use dried seed heads, grasses and flowers. Even if your fresh leaves turn brown, your collage will still be an attractive miniature autumn garden!

5 MINUTES

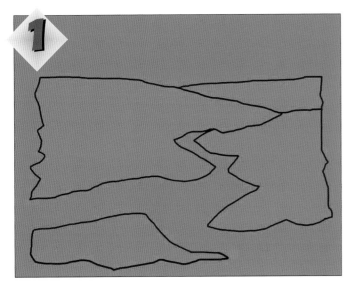

Draw simple outlines for your garden as a guide to building your collage.

Arrange similar objects together to fill areas with interesting patterns and colours.

Fill in open areas with contrasting foliage. Stick each piece down carefully and allow to dry.

Use distinctive elements for trees. Leaves can be used to make bird shapes.

57

Hints and tips

- To add variety to your garden, you can use dried or pressed flowers.
- Use feathers, small shells or stones.
- The landscape on the right is done in crayons. We put in some sprigs of herbs to add interest. We think they look just like trees.

Recycled robot

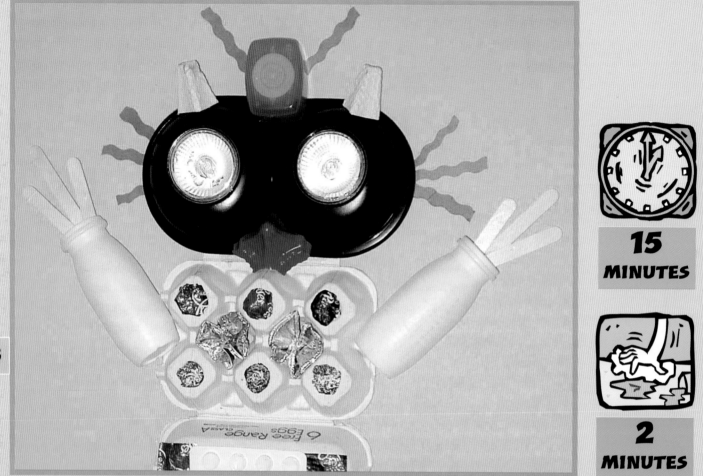

15 MINUTES

2 MINUTES

Bring a pile of junk to life! Robots are all different. Make yours now!

You will need:

- Coloured card for background
- Universal glue
- Assortment of packaging
- Foil containers
- Plastic trays and lids
- Sweet wrappers
- Scissors

What to do...

Look out for old packaging and worn out bits and pieces which could become your robot! Ask an adult for things you can use. We found lots of the things in the recycling bin for this project. Sort out what you have been given. Look for round things which could be eyes. Look for stringy things which could be weird hair. Arrange the bits on your background.

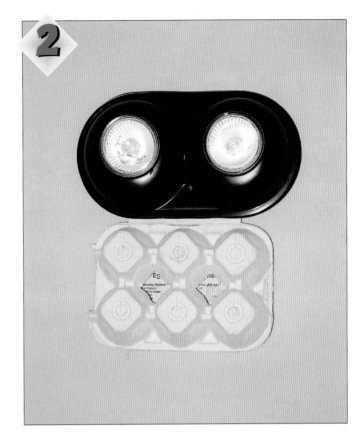

Check which bits you like. Ignore anything too big and think about what will fit on your card.

We used a plastic vegetable tray and two lids for our robot's head. His body is an egg box.

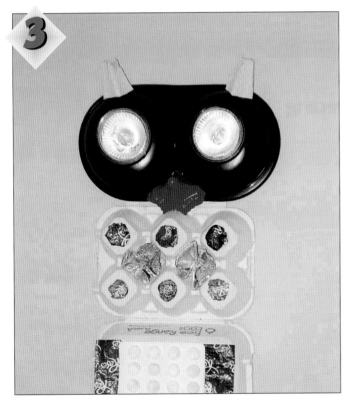

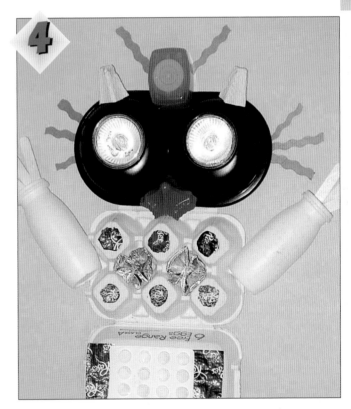

His nose is a red plastic cake tray and his ears are made from bits of egg box.

Small bottles make arms. Finally, he gets wavy-cut cardboard hair and an orange head beacon!

Fish supper

Here's a chance to make an appetising meal in ten minutes! Enjoy!

You will need:

- *Paper plates*
- *Old magazines*
- *Scissors*
- *Glue stick*

30
MINUTES

What to do...

From your magazines, cut out patches of texture which remind you of food. Change the menu to suit the food pictures you find.

5
MINUTES

Take a paper plate. We cut these chips from a big desert picture.

Pictures of a car, a forest and tomatoes make the onion, mushroom and tomatoes.

Add the fish (it's from a jewellery picture) and the slice of lemon (from a fabric brochure).

For dessert, try the ice cream platter (below, left) or a fruit salad (below, right)!

Making faces

Collage is perfect for exercising the imagination. Try using it to make different faces. You will soon create either a beauty or a monster!

25 MINUTES

5 MINUTES

You will need:

- *Coloured card*
- *Old magazines*
- *Scissors*
- *Glue stick*
- *Tray*
- *Waste-paper basket*

What to do...

Search through your magazines for pictures of faces with clearly defined features. You will often find these in advertisements. As you cut them out, use a tray for the cuttings you want to keep so they don't get mixed up with the waste paper. Cut out plenty of pieces so that you have a good selection to choose from. Use coloured card as a background.

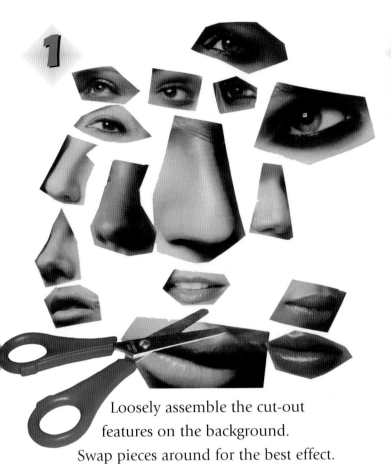

1

Loosely assemble the cut-out
features on the background.
Swap pieces around for the best effect.

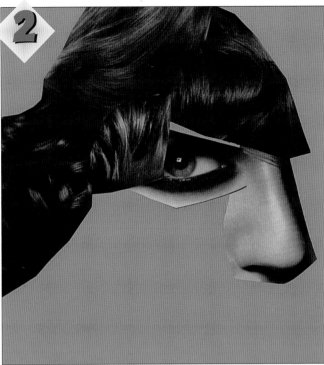

2

As a face starts to develop, carefully stick down
the shapes. Avoid getting glue on the surface of
the image.

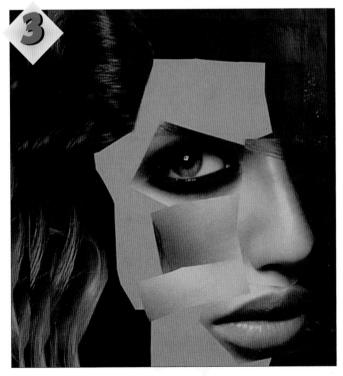

3

Build up the picture with patches of skin colour
and hair textures.

4

Continue to add to the collage until you are
satisfied with your creation!

Wise owl

40
MINUTES

5
MINUTES

You will need:

- *Coloured papers*
- *Seeds or small leaves*
- *Matchsticks, felt*
- *Scissors, pencil*
- *Universal glue*
- *Marker pens*

What to do...

Choose a brightly coloured sheet of paper for a background. Use cream-coloured paper to make the owl's body. Fold it in half lengthways and draw on the head, wing and tail shapes. Cut round your drawing then unfold the shape to reveal your owl. Stick the owl's body in the middle of your background.

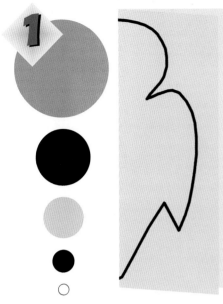

You will need ten circles for both eyes. The largest circle is brown, then black, yellow, black and white. Cut them out from coloured paper or felt.

Stick the eyes on the head of the owl. Add pieces of matchstick round the eyes. Cut a beak shape from some orange paper. Fold it in half lengthways and glue in place.

We have used sycamore seeds for feathers. You could use real feathers or small leaves. Start from the top and outer edges. Stick down each piece, overlapping as you go along.

Concentrate on the wings and tail. Leave the cream centre plain except for some little decorative touches.

Add a few feathers to his head. Cut out some claws from coloured paper or felt for his feet. Glue them on.

Allow the glue to dry. Pin the work on the wall. Your first wildlife collage is finished. Well done!

Cut and tear!

Try cutting pictures from magazines to make faces. In the collage
on the left, we've used pictures that look like other things: the
bananas look like lips, for example. In the collage on the right,
we've used bits of colour and texture. We achieved this effect by
tearing pictures into small pieces and using them like a mosaic.

You will need:

- *Drawing paper*
- *Lots of old magazines*
- *Scissors, glue stick*
- *Pencil*
- *Tray*

45 MINUTES

What to do...

Sort through your old
magazines. Make up two
collections of pictures.

5 MINUTES

1

Find a page with a pattern all over it. Cut out a large oval shape.

2

Search for things that look like eyes, nose and ears.

3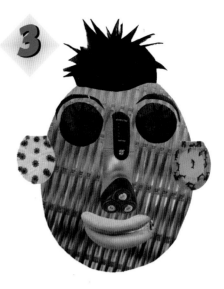

Stick down the oval, then add the features.

1

We made this simple line drawing from a photo of a singer. Use any picture you like, but try a face first. Outline areas of different colours and texture such as eyes, nose, lips, hair and eyebrows.

2

Tear up lots of skin-coloured printed paper from your magazines. The pieces should be roughly 12mm (0.5in) square. Find other colours for eyes, hair and lips. Keep the colours in separate colour groups, like a palette.

3

Overlap the pieces as you stick them down. If you need white for eyes or teeth, allow the background paper to show. For small details, such as eyebrows or eyelashes, cut shapes from a suitable colour.

Moving zoo

Mobiles are fascinating to watch and quite easy to make. They are a good present for a new baby.

35 MINUTES

5 MINUTES

You will need:

- Coloured felt, thin card
- Coloured pipe cleaners, paper clips
- Black thread, sewing needle
- Scissors, fabric glue
- Tracing paper

What to do...

You can make your own shapes or use the patterns on page 70. Trace or photocopy the animal shapes on to card.

1

Fix the animal card shape to the two layers of felt with a paper clip. Carefully cut round each animal with scissors.

2

Stick the felt shapes to both sides of the card. Glue on felt stripes or spots as you wish.

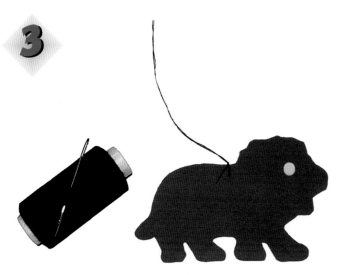

3

Use a needle to attach 250mm (10in) of thread to each animal at the place marked with a red dot on the patterns. Make ten small circles of felt or card for eyes and stick one to each side of the animals. Use two pipe cleaners, 230mm (9in) long, twisted together for the top bar of the mobile. Make a hanging loop at the centre.

4

Use one pipe cleaner, 100mm (4in) long, to make the lower bar. Hang an animal from each end of the top bar with threads about 130mm (5in) long. Hang three animals from the lower bar. Make the threads 130mm, 230mm and 130mm (5in, 9in and 5in) long, so that the centre animal hangs lowest. Use a 100mm (4in) thread to fix the lower bar to the top bar. Ask an adult to help you to hang the mobile.

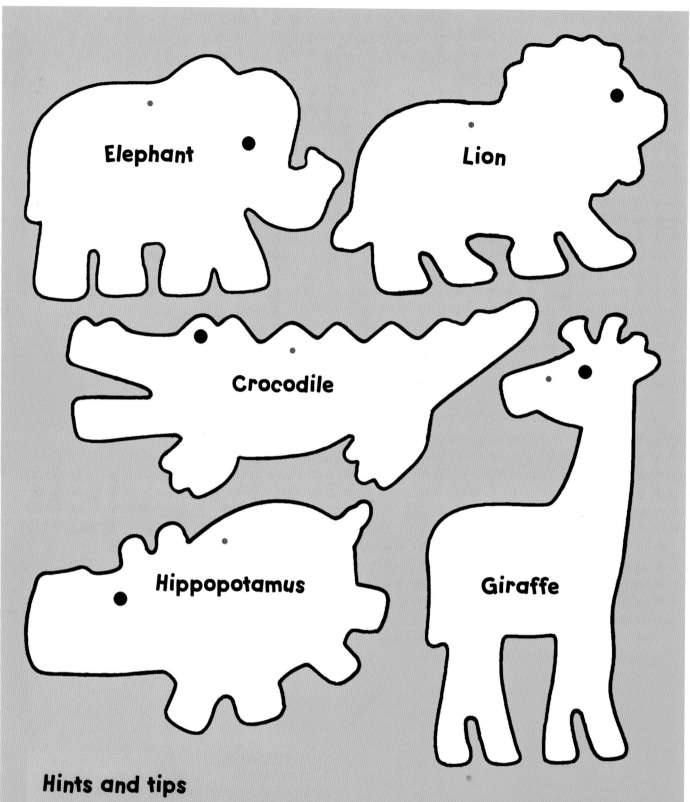

Elephant

Lion

Crocodile

Hippopotamus

Giraffe

Hints and tips

- If you are making different animals, use
  a pin to find the balancing point shown
  by the red dot on the patterns above.

Paper Folding

Windmills

The paper windmill is an old favourite, and very simple to make. Enjoy creating our model with your friends.

10 MINUTES

1 MINUTE

You will need:

- *Thin card or coloured paper, pins, sticks*
- *Scissors, ruler or set square, pencil*

What to do...

From your card, cut out a square 200mm x 200mm (8in x 8in).

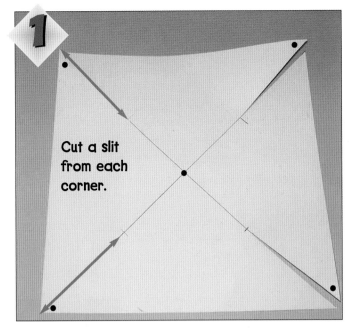

1 Cut a slit from each corner.

Draw diagonal lines from corner to corner. Use scissors to make cuts 100mm (4in) in from the corners. Make a small hole in the centre and to one side of each corner.

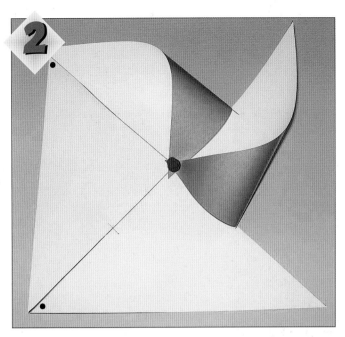

2

Stick a pin through one corner hole and bend the paper in to the middle.

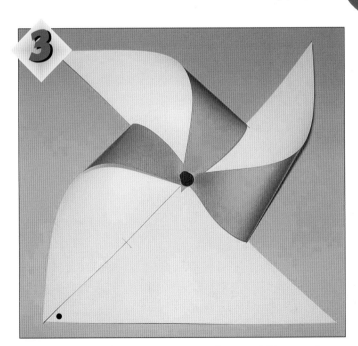

3

Gathered all four corners in the middle, push the pin through the centre hole and press it into the top of a stick. Adjust the pin so that the windmill turns freely.

4

It's best to decorate the paper before you assemble your windmill.

Paper flowers

Make five or six of these lovely paper flowers and put them together in a colourful bouquet for someone you like.

You will need:

- Coloured tissue paper
- Coloured crêpe paper
- Coloured pipe cleaners
- Universal glue
- Scissors, a pencil

25 MINUTES

What to do...

These flowers are made using tissue paper for petals and coloured pipe cleaners for stems. You can experiment with crêpe paper as well.

5 MINUTES

74

1 Fold some squares of tissue paper into quarters. Cut petal shapes out of the unfolded sides. Snip the point off the corner of the folded paper.

2 Open the tissue paper to reveal petal shapes. Cut three different sizes.

3 Fold some squares of green paper and cut into spiky leaf shapes. Snip the point off the corner to make a hole.

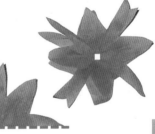

4 Starting with the largest, place the petal shapes on top of one another. Put the leaf shape at the bottom.

5 Use a pipe cleaner for the stem. Fold a small piece of black tissue into a roll and snip it to make a fringe. Wind this around the top of the stem and glue it on.

6 Push the bottom of the stem through the hole in the petal shapes. Glue the leaf shape in place, underneath the petals.

Make leaves from crepe paper. Fix them to the stem with glue.

Make the stem form a spiral by winding it round a pencil.

Party hats

Follow these easy steps to make some colourful party hats – a princely crown and a feathered cap!

You will need:

- *Coloured paper (A3)*
- *Coloured feathers, shiny stars*
- *Scissors, glue stick, stapler*
- *Marker pens, pencil*

25 MINUTES

What to do...

For the first hat, we've used paper that's blue on one side and white on the other to make the folding more straightforward. Fold the paper lengthways to make a crease, then flatten it out again.

5 MINUTES

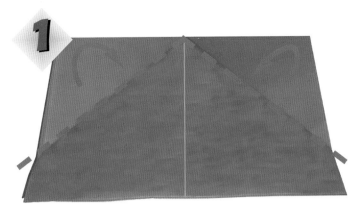

1

Fold the paper short side to short side. Fold the corners to meet the centre crease.

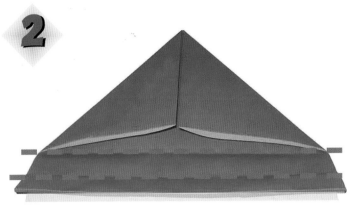

2

Take the strip below the triangle and fold the top layer in half, and then upwards.

3

Turn the hat over, and fold the lower edge as in stage 2. Pull the sides outwards to form the hat.

4

Make a diamond-shaped badge from paper and a shiny star. Tape some feathers behind it. Fix the badge with glue.

1

2

To make the second hat, take a piece of paper at least 450mm x 125mm (18in x 5in). Fold it in half and then fold in half again. Draw shapes and cut them out. Staple the ends of the strip together to fit round your head. Stick on coloured paper shapes to complete the fine crown!

Paper banger

BANG!

These bangers are harmless but can be very noisy! They are easily made from a cereal box and a sheet of office paper. Amaze your friends, but remember to keep bangers away from pets – and teachers!

10 MINUTES

2 MINUTES

You will need:

- Empty cereal box
- Office paper (A4)
- Marker pen, ruler
- Glue stick
- Scissors
- Ear plugs (optional)

What to do...

Our banger is made from two triangles. One triangle is made from card, measuring 380mm x 270mm x 270mm (15in x 10.5in x 10.5in). The other is made from paper, measuring 270mm x 190mm x 190mm (10.5in x 7.5in x 7.5in), with 12mm (0.5in) flaps on the short sides.

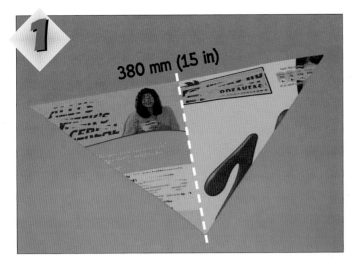

380 mm (15 in)

Carefully fold the card triangle in half.

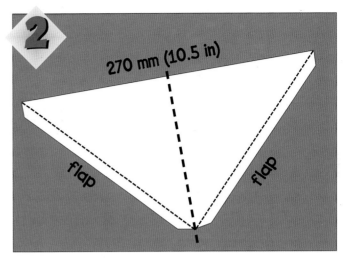

270 mm (10.5 in)

flap

flap

Cut out the paper triangle, including flaps.
Make the folds as shown.

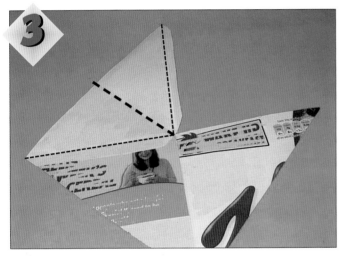

Glue one flap of the paper to the matching
inner edge on the card triangle.

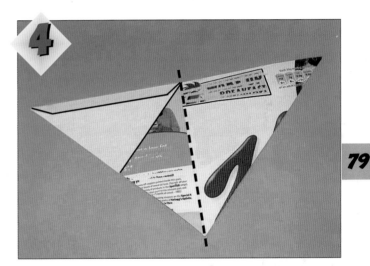

Fold the paper in half and glue down the other
flap. Close the card triangle on top of the flap.

To make the banger work, hold the corner
without the paper and bring it down sharply!

BANG!

A definite result!
Keep away from nervous people!

Snappers

Snappers are quick to make. Once you have the basic shape it's easy to customize them by adding different eyes, eyelashes, nostrils, teeth and tongues. Snappers are spring-loaded and can be animated by opening and closing your hand.

15 MINUTES

2 MINUTES

You will need:

- *Coloured paper*
- *Scissors*
- *Glue stick*
- *Pencil*

What to do...

Choose some really brightly coloured paper to build your snappers. Follow steps 1 to 9. Take care to make sharp folds as you create your snapper. You could challenge your friends to see who can make the most spectacular one!

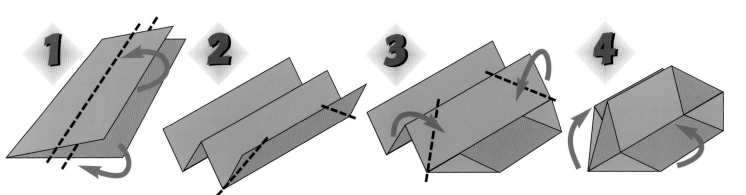

1 Use a square of paper about 200mm x 200mm (8in x 8in). Fold it in half, open out, then fold the sides back to the middle.

2 Fold in the corners of the first section to meet the first fold.

3 Fold down the corners of the second section to meet the same fold.

4 Fold over the corners of the last section to meet the fold on the other side. Bring the sides up.

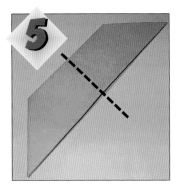

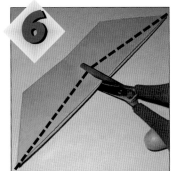

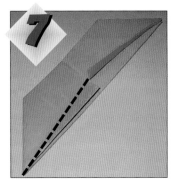

5 Fold the shape in half to find the centre.

6 Make a 12mm (0.5in) cut along the fold.

7 Fold the long triangles back on both sides.

8 Pull the sides apart.

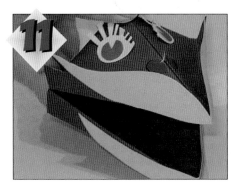

9 Fold it over so that the points meet.

10 Open and close the snapper by moving your fingers and thumb. Stick on eyes, zigzag teeth, nostrils and tongue.

11 Give your snapper different features to make him unique.

Fortune teller

This fortune teller will be popular, as most people are curious to know about their future! Write some really interesting fortunes for your friends and family.

You will need:

- *Coloured or office paper*
- *Scissors, ruler*
- *Marker pen*
- *Stick-on shapes*

10 MINUTES

What to do...

You need a square of paper about 200mm x 200mm (8in x 8in). Follow stages 1 to 5 carefully for a homemade toy that'll bring you hours of fun!

0 MINUTES

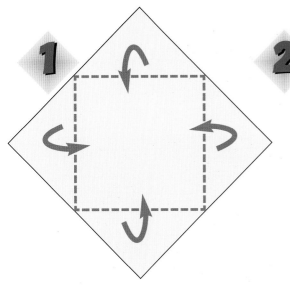

1 Fold the corners of your paper to the middle.

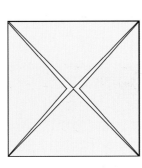

2 This makes a smaller square. Now turn the paper over.

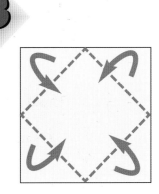

3 Fold the corners of this square into the middle, as before.

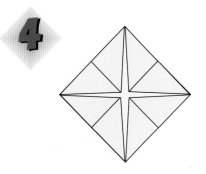

4 Turn the paper over. You should see four square flaps.

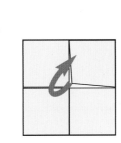

5 Lift the flaps and put your fingers and thumbs inside to bring the four points together (see main picture opposite).

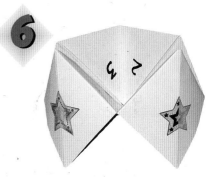

6 Decorate the outside with coloured stickers. Write the figures 1 to 8 on the inside flaps.

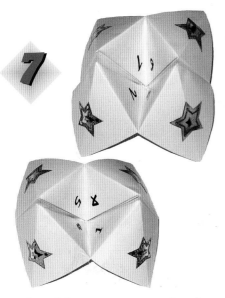

7 Write eight messages under the numbered flaps. Ask a friend to choose a number. Open and

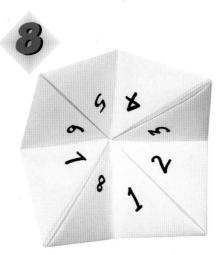

8 close the fortune teller with your fingers and thumbs, counting aloud up to the number. Ask

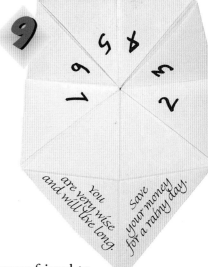

9 your friend to choose a number inside. Read out the message.

Water bomb !

You can fill this clever paper box with water and throw it at a friend on a hot day! It will take you two minutes to make and you don't need glue!

You will need:

- Coloured office paper
- Scissors, ruler
- Tap water

2 MINUTES

What to do...

Cut your paper into squares. 200 x 200mm (8in x 8in) is a good size to start with. It will make a water bomb a bit smaller than a tennis ball.

? MINUTES

1

Fold your square of paper corner to corner both ways.

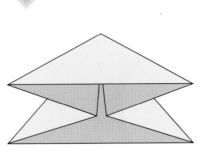

2

Push the sides in so that the paper folds on the creases, making a triangle shape.

3

Lay flat and fold the corners of the top side up to the middle point.

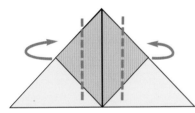

4

Fold over the corners of the flaps to meet in the middle.

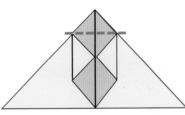

5

Fold down the top points of the triangle to meet in the middle.

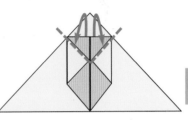

6

Fold the small triangles over again and tuck into the folds left and right.

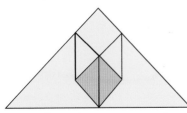

7

Turn the paper over and repeat steps 3 to 6.

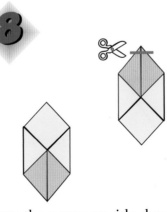

8

Turn the paper upside down and snip or tear off the tip of the point made up of folds.

9

Blow air into the bomb to inflate it. Fill the bomb with tap water and you are ready for testing!

Swan mobile

25 MINUTES

5 MINUTES

You will need:

- White card, scissors, glue stick
- Thin barbecue stick, 200mm (8in) in length
- Office paper, photocopies, tracing paper, a pin
- Dark thread, black and coloured marker pens

What to do...

You can trace or photocopy our templates on page 88.

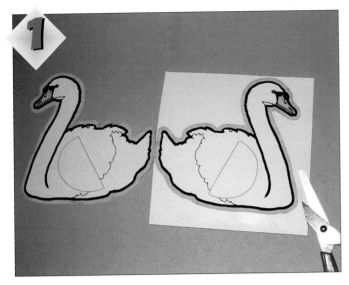

1

Stick a photocopy of the big double swan on a piece of card, or draw the large swan on both sides of card. Work in pencil, then go round the outline in thick black marker. Cut the swans out, leaving a border, which you can colour pale blue. Colour their beaks orange.

2 Cut two wing shapes for each swan from white office paper, using the templates on page 88.

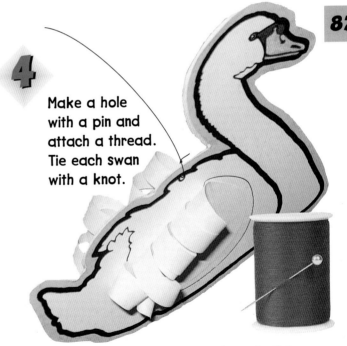

Make four cuts in each wing along the fine lines. Curl the paper by wrapping each strip around a pencil. Make sure your wings are in pairs, left and right. Stick the rounded part of the wings on to the outline patches on the swan.

3

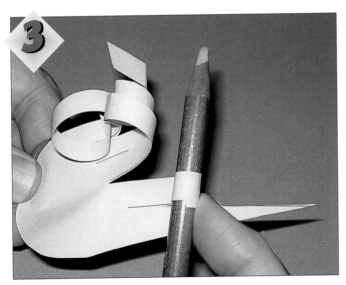

Repeat the process until you have one large swan and at least three smaller ones. A dot on the top of the swan's back indicates where the thread should be fixed. Allow plenty of thread for each swan. Using a short thread, fix the big swan to the middle of the stick.

4

Make a hole with a pin and attach a thread. Tie each swan with a knot.

Suspend one smaller swan at each end of the stick. Put the last swan in the middle, but hanging lower. Ensure all the swans can move freely. Ask an adult to help you. Check the picture on the page opposite.

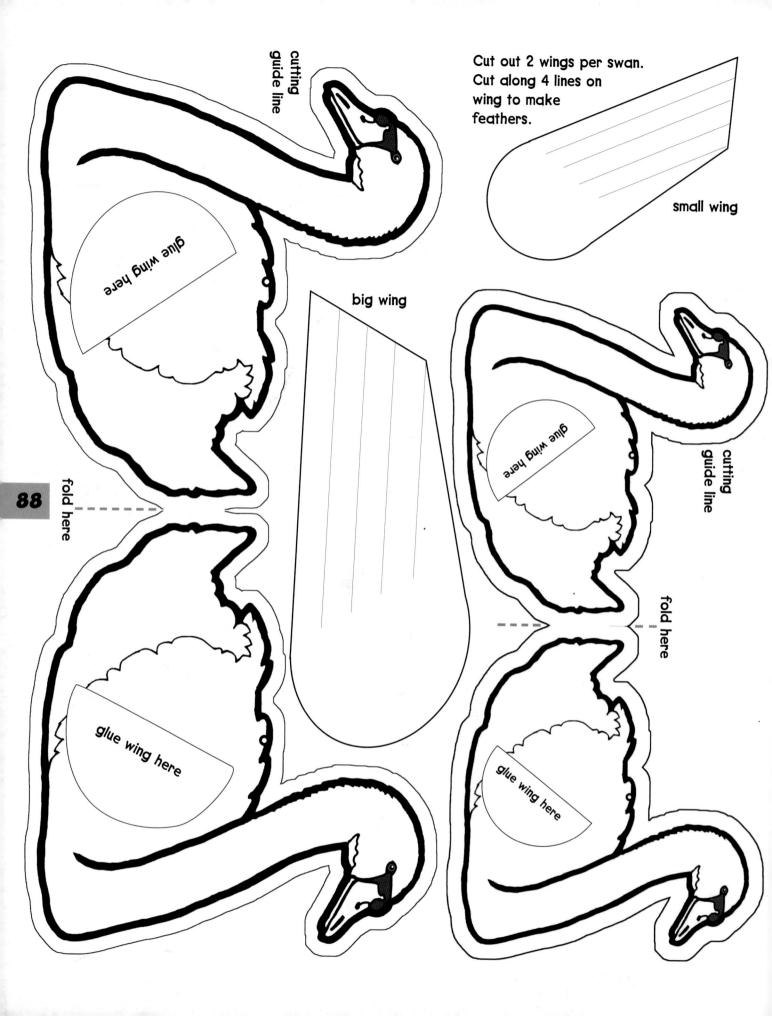

cutting
guide line

Cut out 2 wings per swan.
Cut along 4 lines on
wing to make
feathers.

small wing

glue wing here

big wing

cutting
guide line

glue wing here

fold here

fold here

glue wing here

glue wing here

Card Making

Birthday cake

Celebrate a special birthday with this cake and candles card.

You will need:

- Coloured paper
- Thin white card
- Corrugated paper
- Scissors, glue stick
- Large envelope

35 MINUTES

What to do...

Fold your white card into a tent shape. Use more white card for the candles. Choose brightly coloured papers to make the cut-out shapes.

5 MINUTES

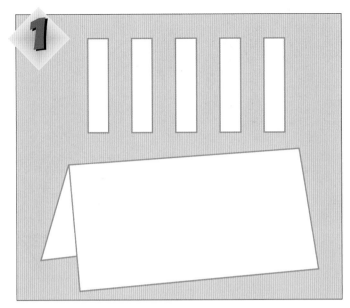

Cut out thin strips of white card for the candles.
Make as many as you need.

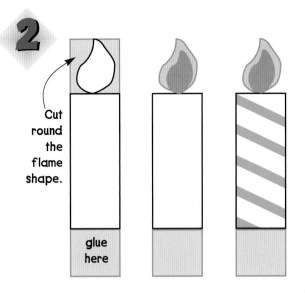

Cut round the flame shape.

glue here

Cut out a flame shape at the top of each candle.
Stick on the coloured paper flames and stripes.

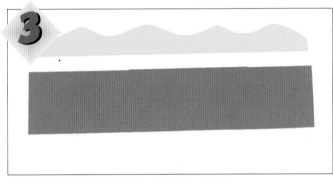

Cut an oblong shape for the cake band and a
wavy shape for the marzipan. Glue them on.

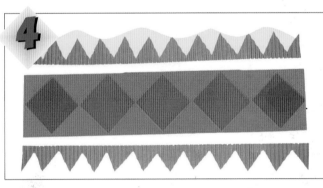

Cut some zigzag strips and diamond shapes
and stick them in position (see opposite page).

Glue the candles to the back of the card.
Space them out evenly. The card is complete!

Write your greeting inside the card. If you need
to make an special envelope, see page 9.

Tortoise and hare

This design is very quick to make, but be sure to follow the cutting instructions carefully! We've made hares and tortoises here, but you can make your cards using any animals you like.

You will need:

- Coloured papers
- Scissors
- Glue stick
- Pencil and markers
- Envelopes

20
MINUTES

What to do...

Always make sharp, accurate folds in your paper. Cut as neatly as you can to give smooth edges to your cards. Make sure you don't cut the joining parts on the fold!

5
MINUTES

1

Fold the paper lengthways in six sections to make a zigzag shape.

2

Draw an outline like this on the folded paper.

3

Keep the paper folded and cut out the shape.

4

Open out your card. Now you need to add some details.

5

Cut out three bow-ties in different colours.

6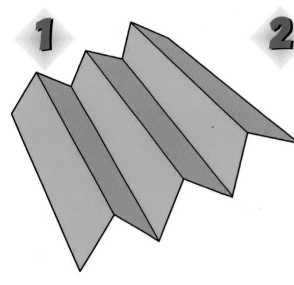

Stick them on. Cut out and glue on noses, eyes and whiskers.

1

Repeat the method – this time for the tortoises!

2

Mark the shapes with a pencil. Cut out with scissors and open.

3

Decorate the shells. Don't forget to write greetings on the back!

Stamp designs

35 MINUTES

5 MINUTES

Stamp designs are simple, quick and fun to make. You can change your stamps to suit the occasion or the person the card is for.

You will need:

- Coloured card, envelopes
- Sponge kitchen cloth
- Plastic lids from aerosols
- Scissors, universal glue
- Marker pens
- Paintbrush
- Poster paints
- Tissues to clean up

What to do...

Draw some simple outlines on paper or directly on to sponge cloth. Our card has frogs, water-lilies and ducks. Copy the templates at the bottom of the opposite page or draw your own designs. Make sure your image fits on the flat side of your aerosol lid. After you have finished, wash your stamps under the tap and keep them for next time.

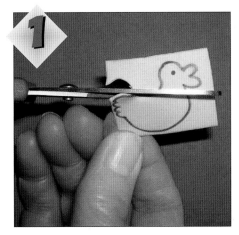

Draw shapes on sponge cloth and cut them out.

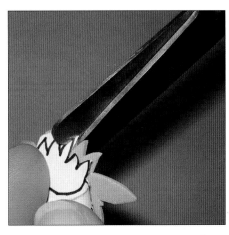

You can use paper patterns if you find this easier.

Stick the shapes onto a plastic lid and allow the glue to dry.

Use thick poster paint to cover the raised part of your stamp.

Turn the lid over and press the stamp on to the card.

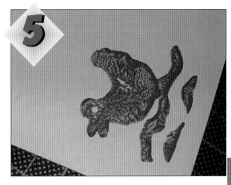

Lift off to reveal the first image. Repeat from step 3.

Work from left to right so that you don't smudge your work (or right to left, if you are left-handed). Let the paint dry.

Make up more stamps to finish your card.

You can use half a potato to make a stamp. Carefully cut patterns on the flat side. Ask an adult to help.

Birthday clowns

45 MINUTES

5 MINUTES

You will need:

- *Coloured card, a large envelope*
- *Scissors, glue stick, a drawing pin*
- *Markers and a pencil*
- *5 paper fasteners, string, glitter*
- *Plastic wobbly eyes (optional)*

What to do...

Copy or trace the shapes opposite on to coloured card, then cut them out. Decorate the shapes with stuck-on coloured paper or draw in the details with marker pens. Check that the completed card fits the envelope.

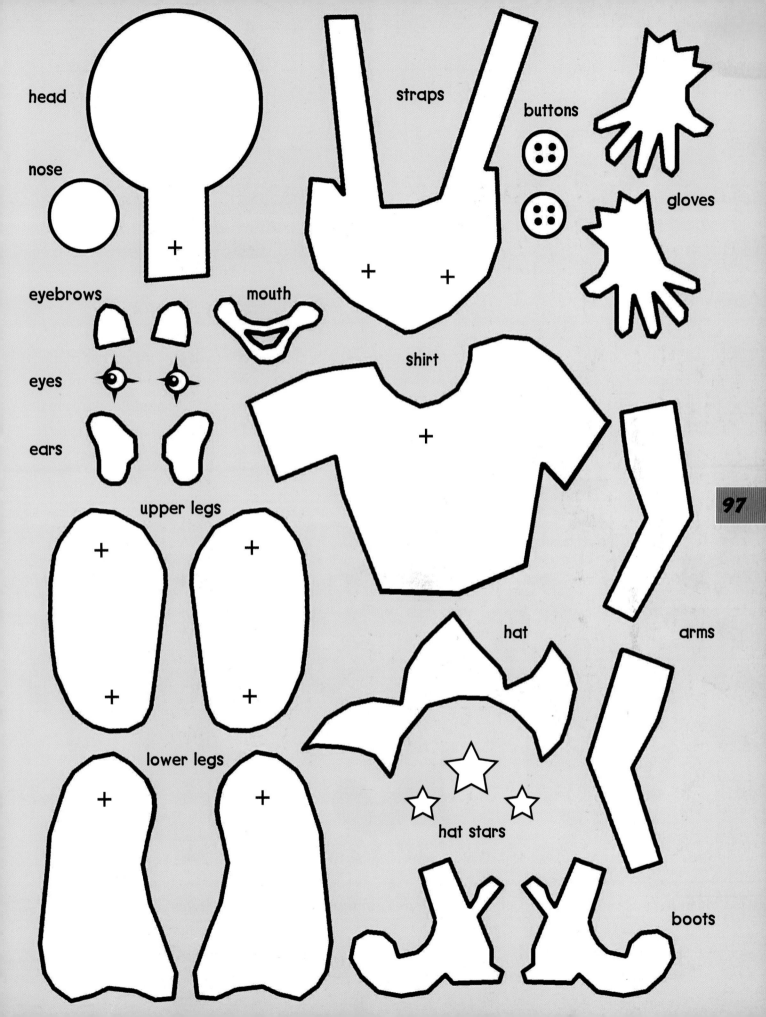

head

nose

straps

buttons

gloves

eyebrows

mouth

eyes

shirt

ears

upper legs

97

hat

arms

lower legs

hat stars

boots

1

Find his head shape and stick his hat on. Glue on his nose, eyebrows, eyes and mouth. Stick on his ears, then put the stars on his hat!

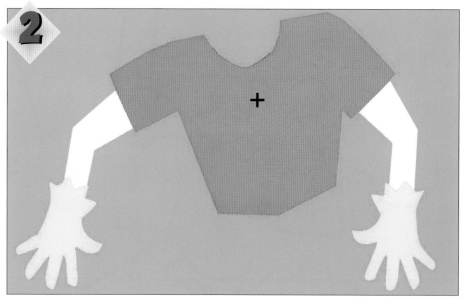

2

Find his arms, two gloves and shirt. Stick his arms behind his shirt and his gloves over his arms as shown. Glue the straps over his shirt. Stick on both the buttons. Allow it to dry.

You will see crosses (+) on the template shapes. These show where you should make a small hole with a drawing pin. The holes are for paper fasteners.

Paper fastener

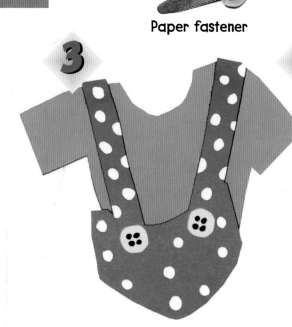

3

Stick his boots to the lower halves of the trousers and point them left and right!

4

Fix his upper legs to his lower legs using paper fasteners. Make sure his joints can move.

5

With more fasteners, join his legs to his body, then fix his head to his shirt. Add a string loop to his hat.

Check you haven't left any pieces out. Write a greeting on the back of your clown. Swing his arms and legs round to fit in a big envelope (see page 9) and address it to your friend.

Fairy   Robot   Pirate

Here are some other faces to copy if you want to make more fun birthday cards. They also make great party invitations. Write the details about the party on the back of the cards. Invent some exciting new clothes for these people to wear. Make templates to show how the pieces go together. Glue and fasten as before. Add some glitter for sparkle. Enjoy the party!

Paper weaving

Happy Birthday

Best Wishes

In a magazine, find a picture you'd really like to use as a greetings card. Then use paper weaving to give it the wow factor!

You will need:

- Thin card, white or coloured
- Marker pens, pencil, ruler
- Coloured magazine pictures
- Black and white photocopies
- Scissors, glue stick
- Envelopes

25 MINUTES

What to do...

Choose a colour picture you like. Find one with a clear image or pattern. Complicated pictures don't work so well.

5 MINUTES

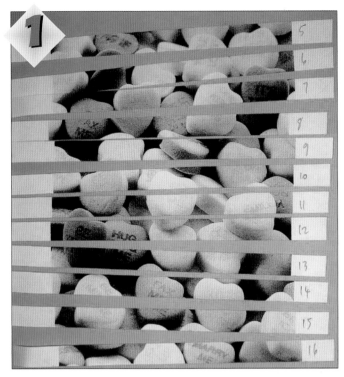

Trim the card to fit your envelope. Take a photocopy of your picture. Cut it horizontally into 12mm (0.5in) strips. Number the strips.

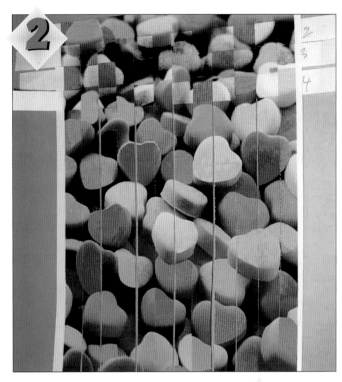

Make vertical cuts 12mm (0.5in) apart in the colour picture, leaving the top 12mm (0.5in) intact. Stick the top edge down on coloured paper.

Starting at the top, weave the strips of the photocopy over and under the colour picture.

Continue to weave the whole picture. Use the numbers to check the strips are in the right order. Now add your greeting.

Opposites

15 MINUTES

2 MINUTES

Opposites – a really quick and effective way to make cards!
Keep to simple shapes and have fun.

You will need:

- *Coloured paper*
- *Thin white card, pencil*
- *Scissors, glue stick*
- *Envelopes*

What to do...

Think of a simple design for your card, or copy ours. Notice that you only need to draw half of the shape. First, fold your white card and trim it to fit your envelope. We found a square envelope for our card, but you can adapt your design to suit the shape of your envelope.

1

Cut an oblong shape in coloured paper, half the width of your card. Draw half the shape in pencil.

2

Cut out the shape with scissors. Keep all the bits of paper together.

3

Glue a different colour paper on your folded card as a background, leaving a narrow white edge. Stick down the right-hand side of your tree first, keeping it straight. Turn the cut-out shapes over and fit them together. Glue them in place. Write your personal message on the inside!

Try other designs using four sides.

Glitter and glue

Exchanging cards is traditional at certain times of the year, especially Christmas. By making drawings in glue and adding glitter, you can make your designs sparkle!

You will need:

- Coloured paper or card
- Marker pens, scissors
- White craft glue
- Coloured glitter
- Envelopes

35 MINUTES

What to do...

Fold and trim your cards to fit your envelopes. For Christmas, you could find a real holly leaf to copy. For Halloween, we have drawn a pumpkin with a face.

10 MINUTES

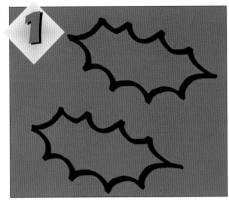

Draw two holly-leaf shapes on some green paper.

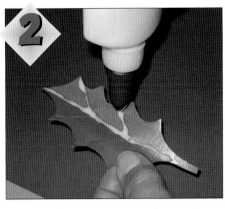

Cut the leaves out and use glue to draw in the veins.

Sprinkle glitter on to the wet glue and shake off the excess.

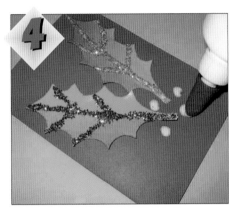

Stick the leaves on the card. Now put some glue and red glitter for berries!

Always allow the glue to dry completely before putting your card in the envelope!

More ideas for cards

- Snowman
- Snow crystals
- Christmas pudding
- Presents in a stocking
- Christmas cracker
- Easter bunny
- Get well soon!
- Valentine hearts

105

Draw a pencil guide line or use glue directly on your card to make an outline of a pumpkin. Add the glitter, and tip off the excess. Put in glue triangles for eyes and nose. Draw the teeth.

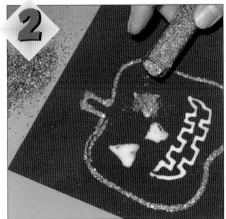

Shake on some more glitter. Let the glue dry. It's finished!

Write greetings inside for your friends. They'll love the cards.

Hints and tips: Work on a big sheet of paper so that you can collect all the dropped glitter for next time!

Pirates ahoy!

Make this unusual card on a pirate theme. It's a complete adventure story in a card!

You will need:

- *Coloured papers, thin card*
- *Coloured marker pens*
- *Fine black marker pen*
- *Scissors, paper glue stick*
- *Large envelope*

35 MINUTES

What to do...

A4 size card is ideal for this project. Fold it in half, short side to short side, then fold it again and again making a zigzag so you have eight sides.

5 MINUTES

1 Look at the templates on page 108. Start with the sea at the bottom of the page. Trace or copy the shape on to blue paper. Cut along the wavy line to make two sets of waves.

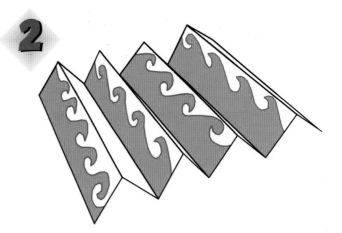

2 Repeat this for four sets. Trim the sides to fit the card. The tops of the waves should be just below the folds. Stick them on the first, third, fifth and seventh faces of your zigzag card.

3 Choose the pirate captain from the templates. Cut him out in card and add coloured paper for his clothes, or colour him in with markers. Draw the details with a fine black marker pen. Glue the tab shown in yellow on the template.

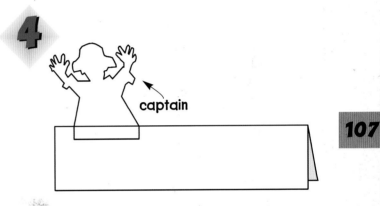

captain

4 Attach it to the back of the first zigzag. Glue the captain on the back of the first wave. Glue the other cut-outs in place. The mate doesn't have a tab. Stick him on the front of the first wave.

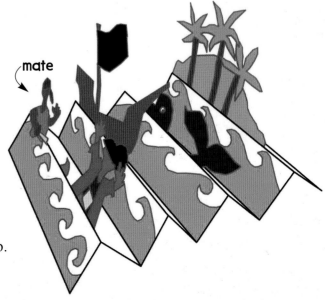

mate

Adjust your card as shown, so that the zigzag stands up. Fold it up to go in the envelope!

island

mate

whale's tail

palm trees

pirate ship

whale

waves   shark's fin   captain

Clay Modelling

Animal parade

Let's model some animals. We've chosen to make an elephant, a piglet, a snail and a little bear – but you can make any animals you like, of course!

15 MINUTES

5 MINUTES

You will need:

- *Modelling clay*
- *Modelling tools*
- *Plastic bag and sticky tape*
- *Plastic wobbly eyes (optional)*

What to do...

Prepare your work surface. Choose your colours and get some clay ready in balls. If you want to make eyes for your animals, make sure you've got some black and white clay.

1   Elephant

The elephant has nine pieces. Make the body, tail and four legs. Now make a head and trunk as one piece. Make two ears. Join the legs and tail to the body. Push his head on and curl his trunk up. Press on both his ears. Add his eyes, and tweak his tail!

2   Piglet

Piglet is made from eight pieces of clay. Make his head and body from one piece. Flatten one end to make his snout. Use clay tools to mark his mouth and nostrils. Pinch the ear flaps before you fix them on. Don't forget to put a twist in his little tail.

3   Snail

Use four colours to make the snail. Roll out brown, white and black into lengths. Twist the lengths together to make his shell. Use fawn clay for his body. Create his eyes from black and white clay. Make a cut for his mouth. Press the shell on to his body to complete the snail.

4   Bear

This little bear is made from eight pieces of brown clay, some black clay for his nose and black and white for his eyes.

Press the arms and legs on to his body. Fix his head and ears. Add a black button nose and two eyes. Shape his mouth with a modelling tool.

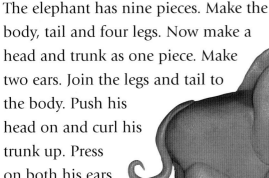

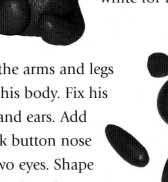

Fridge magnets

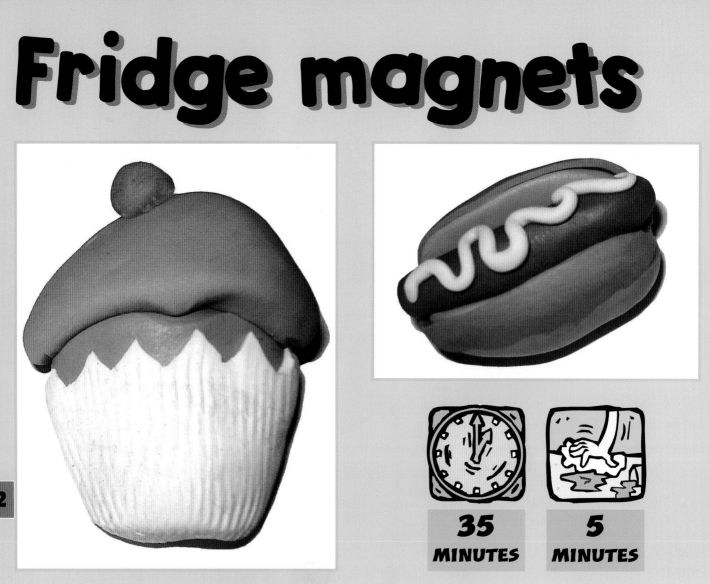

35 MINUTES

5 MINUTES

We made special fridge magnets to stick our shopping lists to the fridge door. They're modelled on our favourite foods, of course!

You will need:

- *Modelling clay*
- *Modelling tools*
- *Plastic bag*
- *Sticky tape*
- *Several flat magnets*
- *Universal glue*
- *Kitchen oven, adult help*

What to do...

Get your work surface ready. Make some clay balls of the colours you are going to use. Think of some fun food items to make. We chose a cup cake and a hot dog!

Create the separate parts from different coloured clays. Find a ridged tool to make the ridges in the paper cup. Assemble carefully.

Make sure the back is flat. When the clay has hardened (see page 10) and is cool, stick the magnet on with a spot of universal glue.

We made the roll for the hot dog out of two colours, then split it, just like the real thing!

You might like some tomato sauce on yours! How about making your favourite snack?

Fashion beads

Clay beads have been worn since ancient times. Follow these easy steps to create your own colourful fashion beads collection.

You will need:

- *Modelling clay*
- *Modelling tools, small knife*
- *Plastic bag, sticky tape*
- *2 lolly sticks, a rolling pin*
- *Cord for stringing beads*
- *Toothpick, a paper clip*
- *Kitchen oven, adult help*

45
MINUTES

What to do...

Choose bright colours to work with. Follow the steps to make the sort of beads you like. We have made three different kinds. You will need about twenty beads for a full necklace. Harden the beads (see page 10) and leave to cool before threading.

5
MINUTES

1

Make two thin strips of clay, 25mm x 50mm (1in x 2in). Put one strip on top of the other.

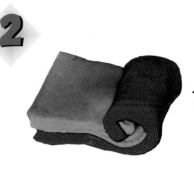

2

Roll up both strips together into a tight spiral. Cut 12mm (0.5in) slices with a small knife.

3

Take care not to squash!

Use a toothpick to make a hole in the bead before hardening.

1

Cut some strips of clay. Place them on a flat piece, 25mm x 25mm (1in x 1in) and roll lightly.

2

Wrap the clay around the thin handle of a paintbrush. Join the edges, overlapping them a little.

3

hardened beads

Ease the beads off the handle. After hardening in the oven, the beads will be firm and shiny.

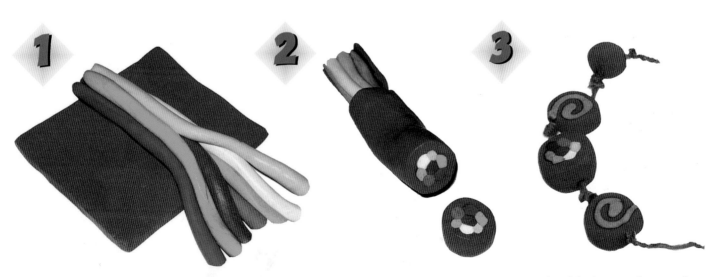

1

Lay bright-coloured clay rolls on a flat piece of clay. Wrap the clay around them, making a cane.

2

Slice carefully. Make a hole in each bead before hardening.

3

Make a double knot after each threaded bead. A loop fastens over the bead at the end.

Friendship bands

It's always great to give something as a token of friendship. By creating your own beads you can make a different band for each of your friends.

You will need:

- Modelling clay
- Modelling tools, a small knife
- Plastic bag, sticky tape
- 2 lolly sticks, a rolling pin
- Shoelace for stringing beads
- Toothpick, paper clip
- Kitchen oven, adult help

35 MINUTES

What to do...

Use colours that look good together. You'll need about fifteen beads to make a wrist band. Make sure your beads have holes before you harden them!

5 MINUTES

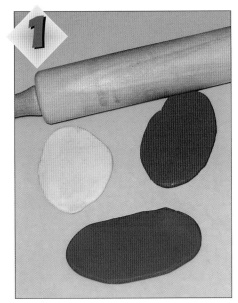

Roll out the clay into thin strips. Put the strips on top of one another.

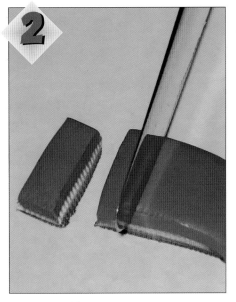

Trim the pile of strips with a small knife. Cut neat slices to make the beads.

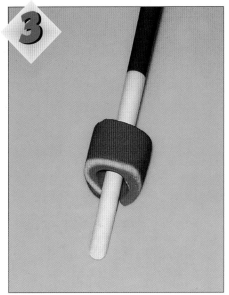

Wrap a slice round a thin handle of a paintbrush and overlap the edges to make a join.

reef knot →

You can vary the shape of the beads by cutting narrow or wide slices. Make round beads by rolling the clay in your hand. Make the hole with a toothpick.

Wrap a three-colour coil round a paintbrush handle to make stripy beads. Look at page 115 for other sorts of beads to make.

Harden the beads and allow them to cool (see page 10). Thread them on a shoelace. Tie the lace with a simple knot so that it's easy to undo.

Picture frame

35 MINUTES

5 MINUTES

If you find plain picture frames a bit dull, here's a way to liven them up!

You will need:

- Modelling clay and tools
- Shaped cutters, ruler
- Plastic bag, sticky tape
- Picture frame

What to do...

Prepare your work surface. Choose your coloured clays. You'll need most for the flat border pieces. Roll out the clay evenly using the lolly sticks (see page 10).

1

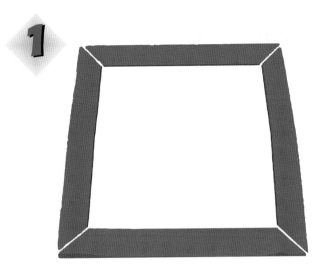

Measure your frame and cut out four pieces of clay to the correct size for the flat border. Make 45° cuts and join the corners. Put the border in place on the frame.

2

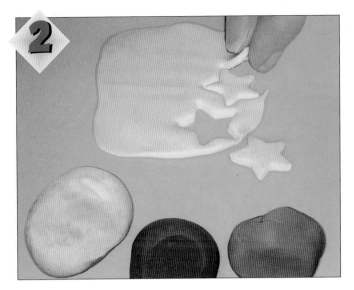

Roll out more clay. Use three or four different clay cutters to make decorative shapes. Plan your design. Work out how many cut-outs of each shape you will need.

3

Press the shapes gently on to the flat border. Build up the pattern until you have worked all the way around the frame. **Do not harden this piece in the oven**. The clay will dry in the air and harden in time.

4

Just add a photograph to complete your new frame! You could try decorating a small framed mirror.

Badge boutique

Badges can mean you belong to a group or club. They can also be given as gifts. Try this project and make badges for your friends and family.

30 MINUTES

5 MINUTES

You will need:

- *Modelling clay and tools*
- *Shaped cutters*
- *Plastic bag, sticky tape*
- *Brooch pins*
- *Universal glue*

What to do...

Think of a badge you'd like to make, or follow one of the methods in the pictures opposite for great results. When the badges have cooled after hardening (see page 10), fix brooch pins to the backs of them with universal glue.

Make a base circle about 25mm (1in) across. Use different colours to make the shapes. Petals go around the edge of the base. Add the green and yellow circles. Punch the edge of the green circle with a matchstick to make a pattern.

Cut a circle for the plate about 40mm (1.5 in) across. Use different colours to make lots of fruit shapes. Place the fruit shapes on the plate and gently press them into place.

Make up each flower shape by curling pieces of flat clay to make petals, then make leaf shapes. Make the base from a small ball of clay. Flatten the back. Add the flowers and leaves to make up your posy.

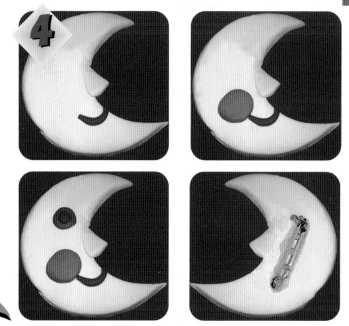

Cut a moon shape from some rolled out clay. Add a fun face. Badges make ideal gifts for parties and friends.

Pencil pals

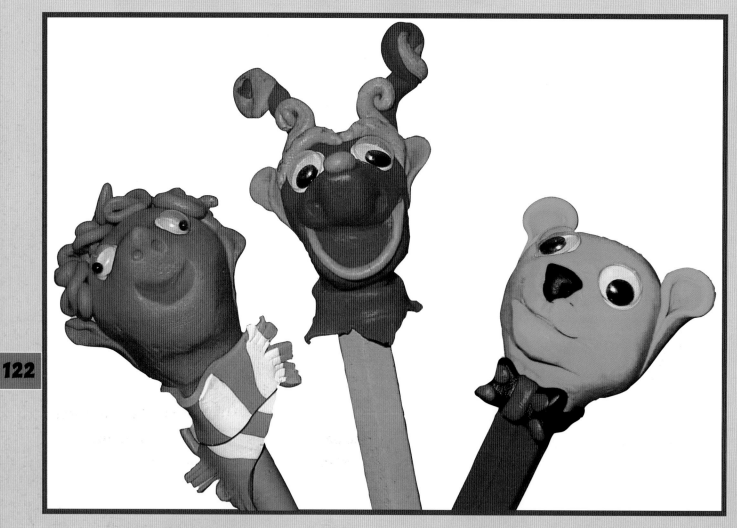

Here are some fun things to make for yourself and your friends.
These freaky faces fit on ordinary pencils.

You will need:

- Modelling clay and tools
- Rolling pin, 2 lolly sticks
- Plastic bag, sticky tape
- 3 pencils, 3 pairs wobbly eyes
- Garlic press, glue, kitchen oven
- Universal glue

**30
MINUTES**

What to do...

We've made three pals. You
need two colours for each. You
can copy these heads or create
similar ones yourself using our
method. See page 10 for
hardening information.

**5
MINUTES**

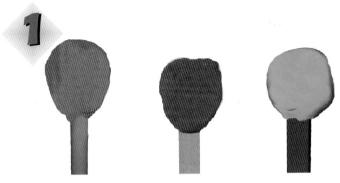

1

Make the clay into a ball and push the pencil into it, about halfway.

2

Roll out more clay between lolly sticks to get an even sheet. Cut out semi-circular shapes and pinch to make ears.

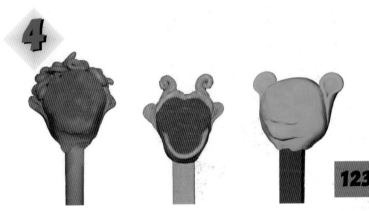

3

A garlic press makes tiny strings of clay, like hair! Twist two strands together to make horns.

4

Make ears and press them on to the heads. Put the hair on, one strand at a time. Add the twisted horns and put on the lips.

123

5

Use clay tools to model the features. Add the noses in different colours. Make a bow tie and scarves. Don't forget the eyes.

6

When you've finished, gently ease the heads off the pencils. Harden and, when cool, stick each head back on its pencil with universal glue.

Clay coil pot

Pottery is an ancient craft. Coiling clay was done in prehistoric times! It's a neat way to make a pretty gift for someone you like.

45 MINUTES **10 MINUTES**

You will need:

- Modelling clay, rolling pin
- Modelling tools
- 1 plastic pot
- Plastic bag, tape
- Shaped cutters

What to do...

Find a small empty plastic food container. This will be the support for your pot. You will also be able to use the pot for flowers.
DO NOT harden this item in the oven!

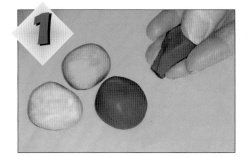

1

Prepare your work surface and some balls of clay. Take some clay and roll it into a sausage.

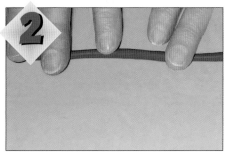

2

Use your whole hand from wrist to fingertips to roll thin coils of clay.

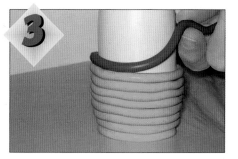

3

Start at the base and wind the clay tightly around the plastic pot. Take care not to flatten the coil. Cover the whole pot.

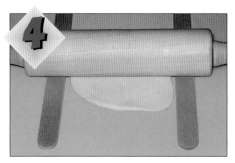

4

Take some different colour clay and roll it out flat.

5

Use a cutter to make shapes to decorate the finished pot.

Once you have wound the coils to the top of the pot, stick the star shapes to the side of the pot. Put some flowers inside if you like!

Pebbles

2 MINUTES

10 MINUTES

Here's an idea that's simplicity itself. Pebbles from the beach? Rare stones from faraway places? We started making them from leftover bits and pieces, and now we can't stop!

You will need:

- *Modelling clay*

What to do...

Find those bits of clay you thought were too small for anything. Combine colours in flat pieces and strings. Experiment and make sure your finished pebbles are smooth.

Glossary

Art board
Thick card with a high-quality smooth surface, often used by professional illustrators.

Cardboard
Boxes for packaging are made of cardboard. It's often dull grey or brown.

Cartridge paper
A thick, rough-textured paper used for drawing.

Corrugated paper
A special kind of board made from two layers of paper with a wavy layer of paper glued between them. It's a very strong sort of paper.

Crease
A crease is the mark left by folding card or paper and flattening it out again.

Crêpe paper
This is a special sort of craft paper made with lots of little wrinkles in it. You can pull it into curved shapes like flower petals.

Diagonal
A diagonal is a line that joins the corners of a square or rectangle.

Diamond-shaped
A four-sided shape, pointed top and bottom and at both sides.

Drawing board
A piece of flat plywood or similar for supporting drawing paper.

Felt
Thick soft cloth which, when cut, doesn't fray at the edges.

Fixative
A clear liquid available as an aerosol for 'fixing' work done in pencil, charcoal, chalk or pastels, to prevent smudging.

Illustrator
An artist who earns his or her living by drawing and painting.

Masking tape
Cream-coloured sticky tape used to put on where you want to prevent paint from going. This is also useful for fixing your paper to your drawing board.

Mobile
A mobile is an artwork that can move. If fixed to the ceiling, they can be hung over a baby's cot.

Mosaic
A picture or pattern made of small pieces of coloured glass, pottery or paper.

Jointed figure
A wooden model with moveable joints used by artists for drawing reference.

Oblong
An oblong is a shape like a square, but longer one way than the other.

Palette
This is a tray or board that you mix up paints in. It can also mean the range of colours that you are using.

Parallel
Lines the same distance apart (like railway tracks) are parallel.

Paper fastener
A small, two-pronged metal item used for fixing papers together.

Pipe cleaners
These are used to clean smokers' pipes. Now there are coloured ones for craft work.

Rectangle
It's the same as an oblong.

Set square
A guide you use to make sure angles are 90°.

Staple
A wire fastener used to fix paper together.

Tab
A small flap of material attached to something.

Template
Sometimes called a pattern, a template is a guide for making lots of things the same shape. We have supplied some for you to use.

Tissue paper
Tissue paper is very thin and is used for wrapping fragile things. You can buy coloured tissue paper from craft shops.

Tracing paper
Thin but strong paper you can see through. Put it on top of something you want to copy and draw on it.

Varnish
A protective liquid, usually clear, for brushing on to finished oil paintings. Paper varnish is also available for drawings.

Index

128